KU-429-839

THE
LIVING
WORLD OF
THE REEF

By HILLARY HAUSER
Photographs by BOB EVANS
Drawings by NANCY LOW

A WALKER GALLERY BOOK
Walker and Company · New York

THE LIVING WORLD OF
THE REEF

STAFF

EDITOR: Jozefa Stuart
ART DIRECTOR: Barbara Huntley
MANAGING EDITOR: Andrea H. Curley
PRODUCTION: David Kellogg
LAYOUT: Karen Bernath

THE SEA AT NIGHT

FRONT COVER:
STARFISH (*Henricia leviuscula*)

BACK COVER:
RED CRAB (*Pleuroncodes planipes*)

PAGE 1:
POINT BENNETT, SAN MIGUEL ISLAND

PAGES 2–3:
POINT BENNETT, SAN MIGUEL ISLAND

All rights reserved under the International Copyright Union by Walker Publishing Company, Inc. No part of this book may be reproduced or transmitted in any form or by any means, electric or mechanical, including photocopying, recording, or by any information storage and retrieval system, without permission in writing from the Publisher.

First published in the United States of America in 1978 by the Walker Publishing Company, Inc., 720 Fifth Avenue, New York, N.Y. 10019

Published simultaneously in Canada by Beaverbooks, Limited, Pickering, Ontario

Printed in Japan by Dai Nippon Printing Co., Ltd., Tokyo

Cloth ISBN: 0-8027-0602-9
Paper ISBN: 0-8027-7130-0

Library of Congress Catalog Card Number: 77-99217

10 9 8 7 6 5 4 3 2 1

CONTENTS

PELICANS AND SEAGULLS ON THE CALIFORNIA SHORE

THE
CHANNEL ISLANDS

The ocean floor off southern California is made up of a series of low depressions and high ridges, created more than 63 million years ago during the pre-Paleocene period. One of these ridges, an extension of the Santa Monica mountain range, forms a unique and exciting group of islands off the town of Santa Barbara, some 90 miles north of Los Angeles. Originally these islands were linked to the mainland by a huge archipelago, but gradual faulting in the earth's crust and consequent changes in sea level led to their isolation. Resident plants and animals eventually evolved into unique species entirely unlike their mainland counterparts. Thus these islands became isolated ecosystems of life.

To give the exact location of the Channel Islands, picture an outline of California. The coast runs along a general north-south axis, but at Point Conception it cuts sharply to the east for about 50 miles. Paralleling this east-west stretch of land lie four islands—San Miguel, Santa Rosa, Santa Cruz and Anacapa. Since they form the Santa Barbara Channel, they are collectively called the Channel Islands. Not in this group but further south lie the islands Catalina, San Nicolas, San Clemente and Santa Barbara. Santa Barbara Island, while far removed from the northern Channel Islands, is usually included with them because, with Anacapa, it forms part of the Channel Islands National Monument, a preserve created in 1938 by the federal government to protect indigenous plants and animals.

The Channel Islands were inhabited for thousands of years by the peaceful Chumash Indians, who lived off the sea and were master canoe builders. The islands were discovered in 1542 by a Portuguese explorer. In 1848 they were ceded to the United States by Mexico; the Indians were wiped out in the 1880's during a frenzied hunt for seal fur. Over the years the islands were bought and leased by various sheep and cattle ranchers. Today some of the islands still belong to cattle ranchers; others are owned by the United States government and still others are maintained as nature preserves. Throughout their changing ownership, these islands have continued to be, above water and below, a wonderful laboratory for the observer and the scientist. While all the plants and animals in this book could, and often do, exist in any one reef community, our photographs come from a variety of different locations among the Channel Islands.

San Miguel

SANTA BARBARA

Santa Rosa

SANTA BARBARA CHANNEL

Santa Cruz

Anacapa

San Nicolas

Santa Barbara

LOS ANGELES

PACIFIC OCEAN

Santa Catalina

San Clemente

0   20
SCALE OF MILES

SAN DIEGO

Opposite: SANTA BARBARA ISLAN

THE LIVING WORLD OF THE REEF

THE
REEF

THE REEF

Until man was able to go underwater, the undersea world had almost always been associated with mysteries and monsters. Then came the development of the scuba tank and regulator and man was equipped with a completely new insight into the life of the sea. Instead of frightening creatures, the early divers found colorful fish that swam around corals and kelp, bright, flowerlike anemones that carpeted the rocks, a brilliant array of hues and a ceaseless activity of life. Today the joy of discovery is still the same for every diver who goes underwater for the first time.

Almost all dives for pleasure, as well as many for science, are made in the vicinity of a reef because the reef is the underwater meeting place for fishes and invertebrates of every conceivable size, shape and color. The reef, by its very nature, attracts and shields marine animals and gives marine plants a place in which to grow. In any ocean, a reef is the chief focus of marine life.

On this ocean-fed, undersea haven every living thing is interrelated and in some way dependent on every other living thing. A reef, therefore, is a perfect illustration of an ecosystem, a word meaning a system in nature in which everything is interdependent. From the tiniest plankton to a five-pound fish, from minute algae to seals and sea lions, all these living organisms benefit from the existence of each other. Remove a seemingly insignificant form of life from the reef and the whole system may go out of kilter with results that can reverberate down the entire chain of marine life.

This vital interrelationship of life is best understood by what is known as symbiosis. Symbiosis, or the living in union of different organisms, is the way of life on a reef. In this world interacting organisms benefit each other very specifically and in so doing create the reef community. Such symbiosis is found, for example, in certain fishes that are immune to the sting of jellyfish. These fishes take shelter in the jellyfish's tentacles, thereby baiting a trap for other fish. When the jellyfish eats its prey, the guest fish shares in the spoils. In another instance of symbiosis, fishes with troublesome parasites allow smaller fishes to pick them off. The pest-ridden fish gets rid of its problem, while the "cleaner" fish gets a free meal. In yet another example, some crabs pick sponges and seaweed off the reef and place them on their backs for camouflage. The crab is then hidden, while sponges and seaweed enjoy a more mobile existence and probably better food selection.

Even the most casual, untrained diver can observe and recognize the interactivity of animals and plants on a reef. To observe, to absorb, to float quietly through water as an outside viewer—this is what going underwater is all about. Firsthand observation has a way of clarifying much of the science and terminology of life in the sea. One begins to realize that animals and plants are classified by their biological particulars and that within specific classes and groupings animals behave in a certain way. Take, for example, the term cnidarian (a term recently substituted for "coelenterate"), which may have no meaning until one learns that cnidarians are simply animals whose bodies form a small sac with a single opening surrounded by tentacles, which usually sting. So this classification includes jellyfish, anemones, hydroids and corals. If a diver looks at coral very closely, he sees little polyps with their tentacles out, feeding. A closer look then reveals that these tentacles sting and paralyze passing plankton, to be caught and eaten by the animal polyps.

We have chosen to illustrate the reef phenomenon by focusing on the waters of California. For one thing, it is our back yard. But for another, more important reason, the marine life of any California reef—whether offshore from the mainland or around an island in the channel, whether in the towering forests of giant kelp or in the tidepools— is unique. The California coast offers a wide variety of underwater environments. There are warm-water areas next to cold-water areas, the result of great geographic variations in the terrain of the ocean bottom as well as unstable ocean conditions and water temperatures that have existed in the Pacific for some 2,000 years.

The animals and plants of a California reef are quite unlike the animals and plants found in the Caribbean. The shallow depths of the vast Little Bahama Bank, for instance, allow more sunlight to filter through the seawater over a greater area. Thus, corals and plants grow more profusely between the patches of sand, and reef fishes have miles of shelter and grazing ground. Off California the contour of the sea bottom is much more varied, and reef communities are correspondingly more isolated from each other. Then, too, deep, dark waters are a tougher environment for plant and animal growth because photosynthesis, the process upon which all living things depend, is directly associated with the amount of sunlight available. There is not much sunlight at the bottom of some of California's underwater canyons, but plankton flourishes in cold water. In fact, the greatest concentration of plankton in any part of the world is found in the polar seas of melting ice. Since plankton is the basis for almost all marine life, wherever plankton abounds marine life abounds. For this reason, the temperate and cold waters of California are rewarding to investigate.

By focusing on an individual reef, one can glimpse a microcosm—a world in miniature—which illustrates and embodies the common principles applicable to ocean life everywhere. Except for the particular species we describe, the reef, as we talk of it, could be anywhere in the world. Though fishes and invertebrates of the world may be called by different names, they are all classified under the same families or groupings, each group containing individuals that have similar body functions and habits. Therefore, the diver who learns that the bright orange California garibaldi *(Hypsypops rubicundus)* is a damselfish (family Pomacentridae) can expect this temperate-water fish to have the same habits as the tropical damselfish of the Bahamas; it is territorial, its eggs are guarded by males during the breeding season and its young are covered with bright blue specks.

The total picture of life on a reef is incomplete without a look at those animals that use the reef above water for resting and breeding yet draw their sustenance from the sea. Mammals, such as sea lions and elephant seals, are important participants in the life of the reef; they feed on fish and crabs, swim about the rocks and kelp, and haul out on dry rocks or sand as they need to. Sea birds also depend heavily on the ocean for food, and pelicans, gulls and cormorants can be seen any day of the year diving for fish that venture too close to the surface. Since these surface reef dwellers contribute significantly to the entire life cycle of the sea, no picture of the world of the reef is complete without them. From open ocean to its bottom of sand and mud, from the busiest underwater community to shallow tidepools—wherever plants and animals interact—this is the world of the reef.

Previous pages: CAVERN POINT, SANTA CRUZ ISLAND
Below: UNDERWATER OFF THE CHANNEL ISLANDS

THE OPEN OCEAN

THE OPEN OCEAN

The sea has many faces. When its mood is gentle its surface is calm and reflects the light of the sun in little diamonds glittering and dancing against a backdrop of blue. When its mood is gloomy the horizon disappears in clouds of gray, sky and sea becoming one. When the heavens break, the sea reacts with tempest-tossed waves that rise and crash as if to devour the earth. For the sailor, the power of the sea both thrills and terrifies. For the dreamer or explorer, the sea is a reminder that there is a vast world beyond its horizon.

This is the surface of the sea. It affects our moods and our spirits. But another drama of the ocean lies beneath the waves, in a world largely invisible to the human eye. To understand all life in the sea, even to know the world of the reef, we must fix our gaze on the open ocean and adjust our microscopes to the mysterious world of the plankton.

In 1845 the German zoologist Johannes Müller, looking for the larvae of starfish, dipped a bucket into the ocean, took a sampling of water and poured it through a fine-mesh net. He found that his sample teemed with microscopic organisms. In further experiments Müller dipped his net directly into the ocean, again with success, and in the end he simplified his technique and merely threw a net overboard and towed it behind his boat.

So, inadvertently, the world of plankton was opened up to science. Müller, excited by his discovery, wrote a colleague advising him to try net towing: "When you have once entered this pelagic, magic world you will not easily leave it again."

The existence of plankton had been ignored until Müller's simple but fruitful net-towing technique became widely known and used. Then biologists everywhere began throwing "Müller nets" overboard and examining their catch. They learned that these microscopic, floating organisms constitute the backbone of all life in the sea and that almost every marine animal and plant exists as plankton in

the early stages of life. Gradually, the life history of thousands of marine organisms began to unravel.

Thirty years after Müller's original discovery, the German oceanographer Victor Hensen coined the term plankton, taking it from the Greek word for "wander." This term was further broken down into zooplankton—animals—and phytoplankton—plants.

Plankton exists in every ocean and sea of the world, in saltwater and fresh, no matter what the water's depth or temperature. Since almost all life in the ocean is nourished by and has its beginnings in plankton, a reef cannot be understood without an appreciation of the role of plankton. Many marine organisms spawn by discharging their spores, eggs or larvae into the water. Once in the water, these tiny organisms drift about, forming the plankton current. As they drift, they grow. At a certain stage, when they have begun to evolve into shapes that foreshadow their adult forms, most organisms leave the plankton. Some then grow into free-swimming animals, some into bottom-dwelling creepers, others into sessile non-movers. The free-swimming organisms are referred to as pelagic and consist mainly of fishes and larger crustaceans. Bottom-dwelling animals are referred to as benthic. The creepers have bodies or shells of such weight that they cannot be independent of the bottom.

Starfish, sea cucumbers and urchins fall into this category and so do sessile attached creatures, like barnacles, mussels, corals and plants.

Jellyfish, salps, some crustaceans (like tiny copepods), algae and worms stay in the plankton all their lives. These permanent drifters include all organisms that cannot propel themselves out of the current. By this definition, some scientists include in the permanent plankton group open-ocean drifters such as the big mola mola. This is the ocean sunfish, which swims aimlessly here and there, never with the power of a fish such as the tuna.

As one example of the richness of life in ocean currents, consider the cabezon, a common fish found off California. One ten-pound female cabezon can lay 100,000 eggs in one sitting, all of which will exist for a short time in the plankton. Some will become larvae; in turn, some of these will become baby cabezons. The rest become food for the other animals. Of the millions of eggs produced by any marine animal, very few survive to maturity.

One way of classifying plankton is by size. Macroplankton is the largest category and includes jellyfish, ctenophores and salps. Then come the microplankton, nannoplankton (nanno meaning "dwarf") and ultraplankton. These smallest plankton cannot be caught with nets; but scientists have learned that they can gather collections of the

Previous pages: CALIFORNIA WATERS
Opposite top: GORGONIAN CORAL (*Lophogorgia chilensis*)
Opposite bottom: BARNACLE FEEDING *(Balanus tintinnabulum californicus)*
Below: MUSSEL SPERMING *(Mytilus californianus)*

tiniest of marine algae by capturing whole salps, which have large amounts of otherwise uncatchable planktonic algae in their stomachs.

From the unobtrusive salp to the baleen whale, plankton is the major food source for all life in the sea. At some point, almost all marine fishes feed on such plankton as copepods, permanent planktonic crustaceans. There are also filter feeders—mollusks, corals, echinoderms and some fish—that siphon seawater through a system of sieves, nets, gills or mucous membranes to screen out and eat the tiniest organisms.

What does plankton have to do with a reef? Everything.

As plankton drifts through ocean waters, if it is not eaten it will eventually evolve into a stage when it must find a suitable substrate upon which it can settle and develop into an adult. Such an environment is one that offers protection, shelter and food —cracks, crevices, rocks, plants, other animals, sea weed, grassy patches, holes and healthy ocean currents.

Artificial reefs give an idea of how a natural reef functions. Anything solid underwater—manmade or otherwise—attracts marine life, and if left undis-turbed becomes a haven for fish and invertebrates. The recognition of this fact came after World War II when ditched airplanes and ships, casualties of war, were investigated and found to be cities of sea life. Organisms had drifted to the wreckages as larvae—algae, anemones, hydroids, corals, barnacles, mussels, crabs, starfish, urchins. Small, larval fish had drifted in and grown into adults. These manmade hulks, now functioning as reefs, offered protection to thousands of marine animals. Bigger, pelagic fish were attracted to these instant reef communities to prey on the smaller, resident fish there. In many cases these artificial reefs have created an oasis of life in the midst of an underwater desert. This discovery led to a flurry of reef—building projects in the hope of increasing aquatic life where it was considered beneficial.

There is no comparison whatever between an artificial reef and a natural one that has developed over thousands of years. Undersea canyons, rocky abutments, underwater mountains, gulleys, ridges, walls, coral configurations, geologic convolutions— a single rock—all these have supported marine colonies long before man was ever on earth.

Below left: CABEZON EGGS (*Scorpaendichthys marmoratus*)
Below right: PLANKTON
Opposite: MOONLIGHT ON A REEF

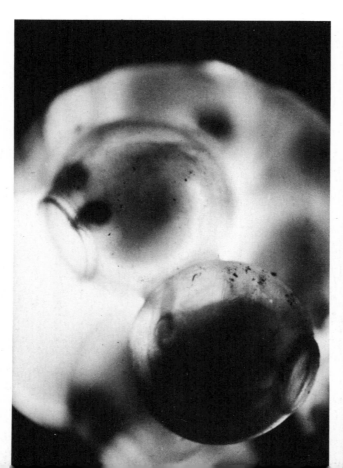

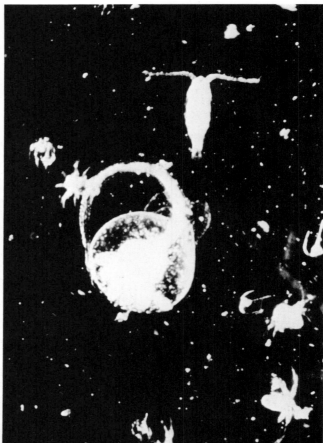

DRIFTERS IN
THE OPEN OCEAN

Jellyfish are among the organisms that stay in the plankton all their lives, drifting with open ocean currents. The purple-striped jellyfish (*Pelagia panopyra*) got its scientific name from its pelagic habits, which have carried this particular species all over the world. While the early development of some jellyfish is considered among the many wonders of the sea, the egg of the purple-striped jellyfish simply grows directly into a free-swimming animal, just like the parent. But there are some jellyfish eggs that, when freed from the parent, drift as larvae until they can attach themselves to something. Once attached, the larva develops tentacles at its free end. When the animal reaches half an inch in length, it divides into a number of tiny, round disks, complete little jellyfish, which are then set free to drift and grow into adults.

The jellyfish is carnivorous. It uses its long, trailing tentacles to sting and paralyze small fish, which it then eats. Some fishes build up a covering slime that protects them against the jellyfish sting and enables them to shelter in its tentacles, since these offer them protection. At the same time, their presence lures unsuspecting animals into the range of the jellyfish's tentacles. In a classical example of symbiosis, the host jellyfish and the guest fish share the spoils.

Below: PURPLE-STRIPED JELLYFISH (*Pelagia panopyra*)
Opposite: PURPLE-STRIPED JELLYFISH (*Pelagia panopyra*)

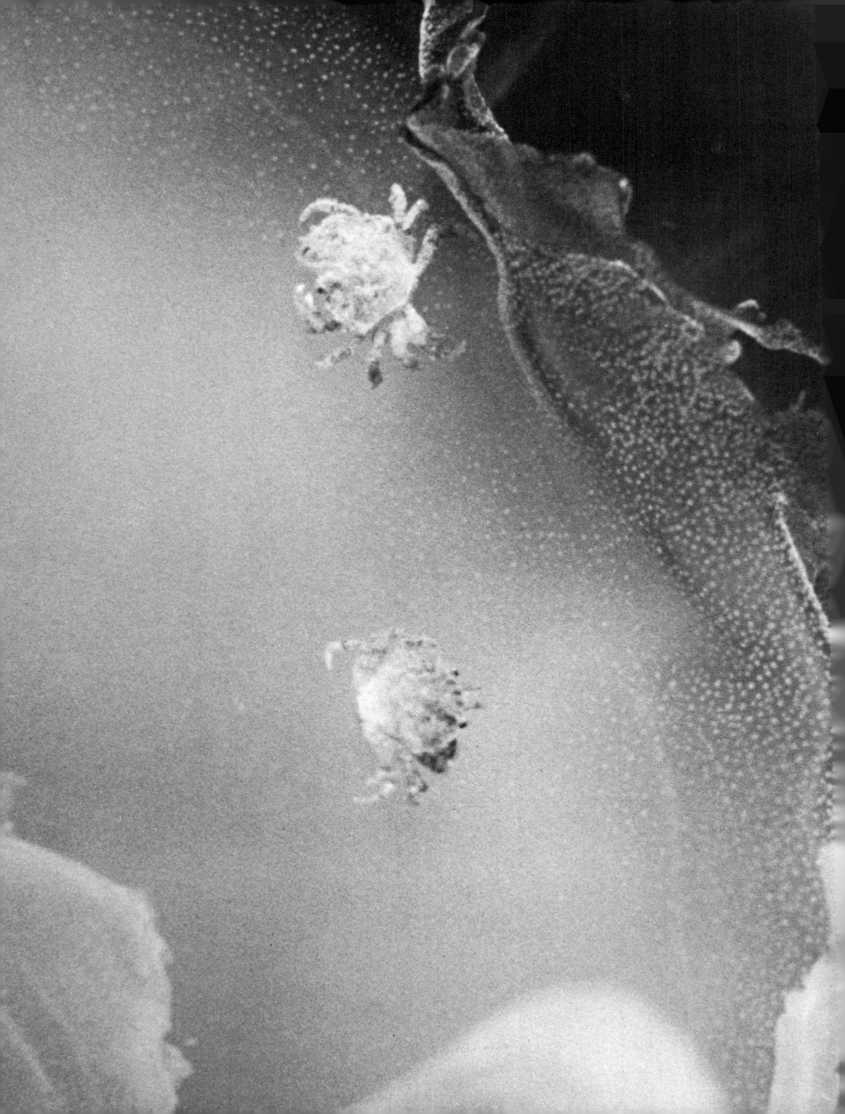

The jellyfish is a cnidarian which, by the simplest definition, is an invertebrate animal with a small, elongated sac and a single opening surrounded by stinging tentacles. What actually stings is the nemocyst, a nettle-cell that can penetrate the hides of fish and invertebrates, as well as human skin. Fish that are immune to the sting are known to have built up their resistance by a gradual exposure to the poison.

The jellyfish sometimes plays host to animals other than the fish. The commensal crab (*Cancer gracilis*), for example, has been known to take advantage of the jellyfish to get a free ride. While the crab is still planktonic larva, it leaves the plankton and settles on the back of a jellyfish, there to grow into a recognizable crab shape. This crab stays with its host until the jellyfish drifts inshore. At this point, the crab leaves and takes up life on a reef.

The disc-shaped jellyfish (*Aurelia aurita*) is found around the world, from polar seas to the tropics. It travels in groups of transparent drifters, usually colorless but occasionally of a light purple or pink shade. Instead of the long, trailing tentacles of *Pelagia*, *Aurelia's* bell only has a fringe of short ones.

Opposite: COMMENSAL CRAB (*Cancer gracilis*)
Below: JELLYFISH (*Aurelia aurita*)

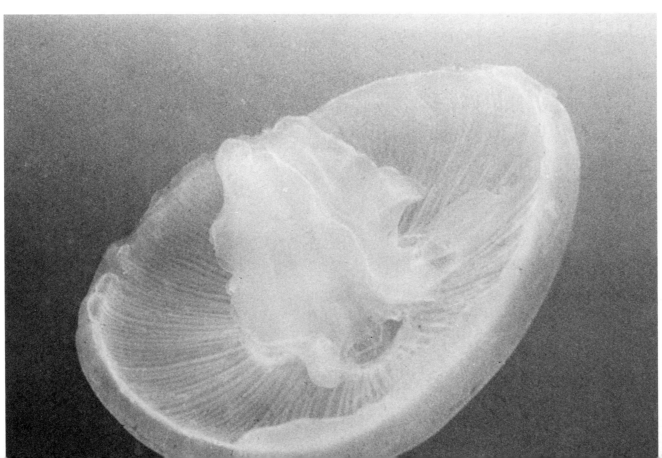

Salps (*Salpa* sp.) are also open ocean drifters, and, like jellyfish, stay with the plankton all their lives. Salps are chordates, scientifically separated from all other animals because a notochord, an elastic rod of cells, forms the supporting axis of their body. They are subclassed as tunicates, animals whose bodies are enclosed in a protective, celluloselike tunic. As the salp floats through the open sea, it siphons water through its body and filters out tiny plants and animals for food. It often has algal plankton in its stomach, so tiny that they cannot be caught by manmade nets. Catching the salp has proven to be the best way to capture this particular plankton.

The transparent tunic of the salp allows biologists to examine its inner workings without dissection. In a unique method of reproduction, the salp is able, very quickly, to form a chain some 20 feet in length, which looks a little like a floating cartridge belt. When the environmental situation is right for reproduction, the organism reacts as fast as it can. Biologist Shane Anderson calls this "a system of opportunity." It is an asexual "budding" process, which enables the parent animal to produce hundreds of new individuals through cell division. Little salps are pushed through the parental tunic, all connected in a chain, all outgrowths of the parent animal. This fast action ensures numbers and thus survival, but it precludes the development of strong characteristics in a species. For this, sexual reproduction by egg and sperm is essential.

The mola mola, or ocean sunfish, is another permanent plankton dweller and, like the pelagic jellyfish and salps, it drifts through all the oceans of the world. It is a poor swimmer and paddles aimlessly. It is often seen floating on its side, hence the "sunfish" tag. The mola mola eats jellyfish, salps, the pelagic larvae of mollusks, as well as some small fish. This big, silver plate of a fish appears to have no tail at all (which is why it is sometimes called a "head fish"). Its generic name from the Latin *mola*, "mill wheel," is a reference to its resemblance to a circular milling stone.

The mola mola is heavily infested with tapeworms and parasites, but "cleaner" fishes, such as surf perches or the blacksmiths (*Chromis punctipinnis*), are quick to attend to this problem. When the big fish drifts into a reef community, more often than not it will be "cleaned" by some obliging, smaller fish. It is a happy solution: the mola mola gets rid of the little parasites that cause trouble if left unchecked, and the cleaners get a free meal.

Below left: SALP (*Salpa* sp.)
Below right: SALP (*Salpa* sp.)
Opposite: OCEAN SUNFISH (*Mola mola*)

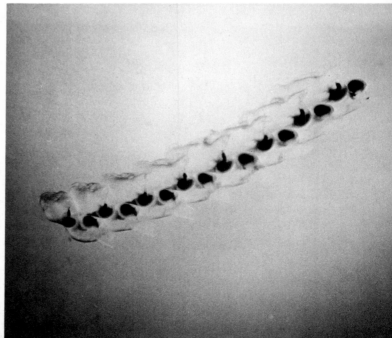

LIFE
UNDERWATER

SCAVENGERS OF
THE OCEAN BOTTOM

The bottom of the ocean is either an underwater desert or a haven of life. The key is sunlight. All growth in the sea depends on the amount of sunlight filtered through the water. Algae and sea plants need light for the process of photosynthesis, by which they manufacture their own food. In turn, fish and other organisms, feeding on these plants, acquire the energy they need for their growth and survival.

On every reef, whether deep and dark or shallow and sunny, there are always scavengers. These animals, sea urchins and sea cucumbers among them, forage for food over rocks and rubble, sand and mud, living on the debris that collects on the bot-

tom, for the most part dead animal matter, or detritus. These bottom creatures provide an important janitorial service for the reef.

Sea urchins, the porcupine balls of the reef, are echinoderms, "spiny skins." These globular pincushions are found everywhere, in shallow water or deep, in sand and rock, among kelp and in tidepools. They prefer rocky areas. They creep around, using little sucker feet and their bristling spines for locomotion, and graze on algae and seaweed, for which they have a ravenous appetite. Once all available vegetation is eaten they turn carnivorous and consume sessile filter-feeders. The notorious spines of the sea urchin ward off predators and also

help catch pieces of kelp, which the animal then eats. The sea urchin (*Strongylocentrotus franciscanus*) is the largest species along the Pacific coast. It can be either of two colors, red-brown or dark purple.

Sea pens (*Stylatula elongata*) are bottom-dwelling, coral-related animals that do not look like animals at all but instead resemble oceanic quills. The "stalk" of the sea pen is embedded in sand or mud, and individual animal polyps grow out of the "rachis." Some polyps (autozooids) take in planktonic food, while the others (siphonozooids) siphon water in and out. The sea pen can withdraw quickly and totally into its hole.

Their defense mechanism rests on an ability to eject their internal organs whenever they are threatened. This visceral mass is poisonous to predators, while the sea cucumber has the ability to regenerate new organs within six to eight weeks.

Sea cucumbers are bottom-dwelling echinoderms, but their spines are less obvious than those of other echinoderms. They are cylindrical in shape and resemble the cucumber, and have leathery, warty skins. Embedded in the skin are tiny calcareous plates. The animals move around sluggishly on tube feet and also through contractions of their bodies. Their diet consists of any detritus or organic matter they can find in sand, mud or rocks.

Previous pages: SEA URCHIN (*Strongylocentrotus franciscanus*)
Opposite top: SEA PENS (*Stylatula elongata*)
Opposite bottom: SEA CUCUMBER (*Parastichopus parvimensis*)
Below: GORGONIAN CORAL (*Lophogorgia chilensis*)

BRILLIANT BLOOMS
ROOTED IN THE SEABED

Anemones are often called the flowers of the sea since they brighten almost every reef in the world. They live in sand or on rocks, wherever they can feed on fish, mollusks or crustaceans, which they catch with their tentacles and paralyze with stinging cells. Anemones, with their single, elongated sac and tentacle-fringed opening, are cnidarians. They are classed as Anthozoa; in Greek *anthas* means "flower" and *zoa* means "animal"—thus, flower animal.

Most anemones are hermaphrodites, animals in which both egg and sperm are present. Anemones can reproduce in several different ways: either sexually, for which they require fertilization by another anemone, or asexually, by budding or splitting apart. The chosen method of reproduction usually depends upon environmental stimulus. For example, there is one anemone that will reproduce by splitting apart until its surroundings are crowded with individuals of its own species, whereupon it changes from asexual reproduction to sexual.

Not only anemones but also mussels, starfish and other lower animals reproduce sexually by discharging eggs and sperm into the water to travel in the ocean currents. The great question then is, how do these microscopic organisms find each other in the great, wide ocean? The answer lies in a hormone. Each egg and sperm has a hormone attached to it, and as the ocean currents carry them over a reef, the hormone triggers animals to release their eggs and sperm in turn.

Groups of genetically identical anemones, growing in colonies and reproduced by an asexual budding process, are called clones. Clones are territorial. When two clones border on each other they push and fight, waving their tentacles, stinging and paralyzing. Nettlelike nematocysts in the tentacles inject the poison that paralyzes foe or prey. Tiny darts filled with venom are discharged from cell to victim, killing or stunning an opposing anemone or the plankton or fish that the anemone needs as food.

Club anemones (*Corynactis californica*) are colonial. They are named for the little white clubs at the end of their tentacles. It is these clubs that contain the nematocysts. Club anemones are a striking blood-red but can also be pink, orange, lavender or white. Their tentacles are always white.

A solitary species, the strawberry anemone (*Tealia crassicornis*) is so named for its appearance when it folds up. The burrowing anemone (*Cerianthus* sp.) builds itself a protective tubular encasement of mucus, stiffened by the interweaving of nematocysts. This tube can sink 3 or 4 feet into the sea bottom and the anemone lives unattached inside. When threatened by predators, the anemone slides to the bottom of its tubing.

Below left: CLUB ANEMONE (*Corynactis californica*)
Below right: STRAWBERRY ANEMONE (*Tealia crassicornis*)
Opposite: BURROWING ANEMONE (*Cerianthus* sp.)

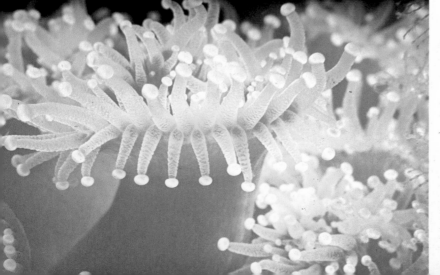

SEA SLUGS
CLOTHED IN VIBRANT COLORS

Nudibranchs are beautiful, delicate sea slugs that come in such a wide variety of vibrant colors that an artist would have a hard time duplicating them. These animals are shell-less mollusks (sometimes referred to as "naked snails") that do not have true gills. They breathe through a network of secondary gills, which are elaborately arrayed on the animal's back, or through the body surface itself. The word *nudibranch* means "naked lung." Nudibranchs prefer shallower waters, where they undulate gracefully in the currents and lay their millions upon millions of eggs.

Hermissenda crassicornis is a colorful nudibranch that swims by doubling and twisting its body. There is always some variation in the color of this nudibranch; it can be yellow-green, bluish gray, or a brick-red, with a blue line down the back. The *cerata* can be brown, red or blue, tipped with yellow. The hermissenda nudibranch eats hydroids and anemones. In some nudibranchs the nematocysts are processed through the system of the animal to give the body the ability to sting.

Hermissenda lays its eggs in almost geometric masses, but the bright lemon nudibranch (*Anisodoris nobilis*) lays its eggs in an even more orderly construction to look like a flower. The lemon nudibranch is a beautiful yellow, mottled with dark brown or black spots between the little knobby tubercles on the animal's back. It has a different gill arrangement from hermissenda—a feathery tuft near its rear that looks almost like a fancy hat. It can withdraw this instantly if alarmed. The lemon nudibranch eats sponges and has a penetrating fruity odor, which is rather strong in its concentrated form. It is believed that this wards off predators.

Opposite top: NUDIBRANCH EGGS (*Hermissenda crassicornis*)
Opposite center: LEMON NUDIBRANCH EGGS (*Anisodoris nobilis*)
Opposite bottom: LEMON NUDIBRANCH (*Anisodoris nobilis*)
Below: NUDIBRANCH (*Hermissenda crassicornis*)

CANNIBALS WITH
A HEALTHY APPETITE

Starfish are carnivorous and eat shellfish, barnacles, mussels, dead fish or invertebrates, jellyfish—and sometimes even smaller versions of themselves. They hold their prey with their long tubular feet and then enclose it with their protruding stomachs. The healthy appetite of the starfish makes it one of the most important scavenger animals of the ocean bottom, in company with the sea urchin and the sea cucumber. Starfish are particularly abun-

dant along the northern Pacific coast. Among the most striking is *Pycnopodia helianthoides*, commonly called the sunflower-star for its fifteen to twenty-four legs. It is among the biggest and fastest moving of all starfish. The bright red *Mediaster aequalis* exists deep underwater. At the very bottom of the ocean, massed varieties of starfish devour a clump of mussels.

Opposite top: STARFISH (*Mediaster aequalis*)
Opposite bottom: SUNFLOWER-STAR (*Pycnopodia helianthoides*)
Below: MASSED STARFISH

Starfish are echinoderms that are classed scientifically as *asteroidea*. This name is derived from the Greek *aster*, meaning "star." The typical starfish has five arms, or rays, but there are some that have more than twenty. Starfish live on the bottom and creep about on little tube feet, preying and grazing on just about everything. The backs of starfish are covered with stubbly spines and some have tiny pincers that open and close; these keep away algae and other organisms that could interfere with the animal's breathing organs. The pincers may also help in the gathering of food. If a tiny organism ventures across the back of a starfish, these pincers can grab the animal and hold it until it can be eaten.

Starfish at times show great ingenuity in the procurement of food. A *Pisaster giganteus* clings by one leg to an overhang and in the other legs holds a scallop that it has pulled off the reef.

Opposite: GIANT SEA STAR (*Pisaster giganteus*)
Below: SUNFLOWER-STAR (*Pycnopodia helianthoides*)

Starfish are territorial and often fight each other for space and for food. Sea bats (*Patiria miniata*) struggle slowly for mastery and a diver, observing them, would have a long wait before seeing either one the victor. The sea bat is named for its webbed rays and it ranges in color from bright red to purple or green. Starfish come in many different vibrant colors. The leather star (*Dermasterias imbricata*) has a smooth skin with a leathery feel to it, and its colors vary from yellow to orange to lead blue. *Pisaster giganteus* has giant white spines on its back, ringed with blue.

Below top: SEA BATS (*Patiria miniata*)
Below bottom: LEATHER STAR (*Dermasterias imbricata*)
Opposite: GIANT SEA STAR (*Pisaster giganteus*)

MASTERS OF DISGUISE
IN THE SEASCAPE OF THE REEF

All reefs shelter animal oddities and prominent among them are the octopus, and the scorpionfish. The octopus (*Octopus bimaculatus*) is a shy little creature and a master of disguise. It has the talent, which it owes to thousands of tiny color cells lodged in the skin, to mix and match its colors to blend with the surroundings. It hides by day and feeds by night, poking into every crack and crevice for food. The octopus opens a bivalved animal, a clam or a mussel, by using its arms or by drilling through the shell with its radula. It then injects venom into its prey, which dies and opens. By forcing a jet of water through its siphon structure, an alarmed octopus can move at lightning speed.

Below: OCTOPUS (*Octopus bimaculatus*)
Opposite: SCORPIONFISH (*Scorpaena guttata*)

This animal is a cephalopod, or "head foot." It is a highly evolved mollusk whose formerly clumsy foot has grown into a more useful head, complete with tentacles and arms.

The scorpionfish (*Scorpaena guttata*) is a spiny, bumpy, mottled, blotched rockfish that can change colors swiftly and disappear into the background. As its name implies, the spines of this fish are capable of inflicting extremely painful wounds on humans and are used against predators. Next to its camouflaging abilities, these spines are the scorpionfish's best defense.

NIGHTTIME FORAGERS
OF THE UNDERWATER WORLD

The electric ray (*Torpedo californica*) is a bottom-dwelling fish that buries itself in the sand by day and cruises around the reef at night in search of prey. It eats small fish, which it captures by delivering a healthy shock. Its electrical powers may also include sensors, with which it picks out bottom fish to attack.

The marine eels of the world are much maligned. They are hardly as ferocious as they are made out to be. In fact, by day they retreat passively into their rocky shelters. The California moray (*Gymnothorax mordax*) is rather bashful, though the generic name *mordax* means "prone to bite." The way it breathes is no doubt responsible for the eel's fierce reputation; as it inhales and exhales, the mouth opens and closes to reveal numerous sharp teeth. The moray's favorite diet does not include human fingers but octopus, squid and crabs, all animals that, like the moray, hide by day and forage at night.

Below: ELECTRIC RAY (*Torpedo californica*)
Opposite: MORAY EEL (*Gymnothorax mordax*)

GLISTENING JEWELS
IN AN OCEAN LANDSCAPE

Mollusks, by definition, are animals with soft bodies protected, in most cases, by a hard shell. All mollusks have a muscular "foot," which they use for clinging to a reef or a rock and also for locomotion. As a general rule, an external shell indicates that the animal inside is a mollusk, but there are important exceptions to this. The octopus and the squid (whose muscular feet have evolved into a head with tentacles), nudibranchs and sea hares are all mollusks without shells.

The high-spired, thick-shelled Kellet's whelk (*Kelletia kelletii*) is a scavenger that feeds on dead animals. The Kellet's whelk lays its eggs in clusters. When the offsprings hatch, they leave the eggs as miniature replicas of an adult.

The red abalone (*Haliotis rufescens*) is the prized catch of sport and commercial divers. The big foot of the abalone is widely marketed as steaks, a seafood delicacy, and the pearly shells of the abalone are big and beautiful. Of all the abalone species found off California, the red abalone has the largest shell, reaching over 11 inches in diameter. The shell is brick-red in color with occasional white stripes, rimmed with a red margin on the underside and punctuated with three or four raised holes. Natural predators of the abalone include the sea otter, cabezon, cancer crab and the octopus.

The chestnut cowry (*Cypraea spadicea*) has a glossy, egg-shaped shell, brown on top and bluish-white on the bottom. A toothed opening extends along the length of the shell. The cowry lives in rocky areas, where it grazes on algae and sponges. Sometimes it congregates in numbers out on a reef. The beautiful shell of a living cowry is often completely covered by a slimy mantle. This may protect the cowry from predatory starfish and may also account for the natural shininess of its shell. The chestnut cowry exists as a bottom scavenger, and one of the animals it preys on is the sea pen, (*Tylosarcus* sp.).

The ringed top shell (*Calliostoma annulatum*) is a small, brilliant underwater jewel. It is gold and has little, flattened whorls decorated with beaded spiral ridges rimmed with purple.

Below: RINGED TOP SHELL (*Calliostoma annulatum*)
Opposite top: KELLET'S WHELK (*Kelletia kelletii*)
Opposite center: RED ABALONE (*Haliotis rufescens*)
Opposite bottom: CHESTNUT COWRY (*Cypraea spadicea*)

FEEDERS ON
THE PASSING PLANKTON

Filter feeders have a marked effect on the overall ecology of a reef and on the plankton current. The larvae produced by millions of local reef animals make up a large part of the plankton current that passes over their own area. Reef residents enjoy a continual banquet, their little feelers and tentacles reaching out into the currents to catch, sting and trap. Their intake of plankton is so great that by the time the passing water mass reaches the downcur-

rent area of a reef the water is significantly depleted. Up-current creatures get the best supply.

The barnacle (*Balanus tintinnabulum californicus*) is not a mollusk but a crustacean, a fact that often surprises people. It is the only crustacean (other than parasitic species) that, as an adult, renounces all freedom of movement and attaches itself to solid objects. When the larva leaves the plankton, the developing shrimplike animal, still

Below: BARNACLE (*Balanus tintinnabulum californicus*)
Opposite: ROCK SCALLOP (*Hinnites giganteus*)

free-swimming, goes through a series of molts. Then it attaches itself, head on, to something firm and hard—a spot on a reef, another hard-shelled animal, a boat bottom—and grows into an adult barnacle with a volcano-shaped shell. Feathery feelers, which are actually the feet of the inverted animal, twist in the passing currents and fan food through the barnacle's tiny doorway.

The rock scallop (*Hinnites giganteus*) is a mollusk so encrusted with other kinds of sea growth that it might go completely unnoticed but for its orange "lips," or mantle. The young scallop has a nearly symmetrical shell and swims freely, but as it grows older, it settles down on a reef in an area that is rocky or bumpy. After it is attached the scallop grows a new, less symmetrical shell, to match its environment. On the inside the shell is white with a purple stain near the hinge.

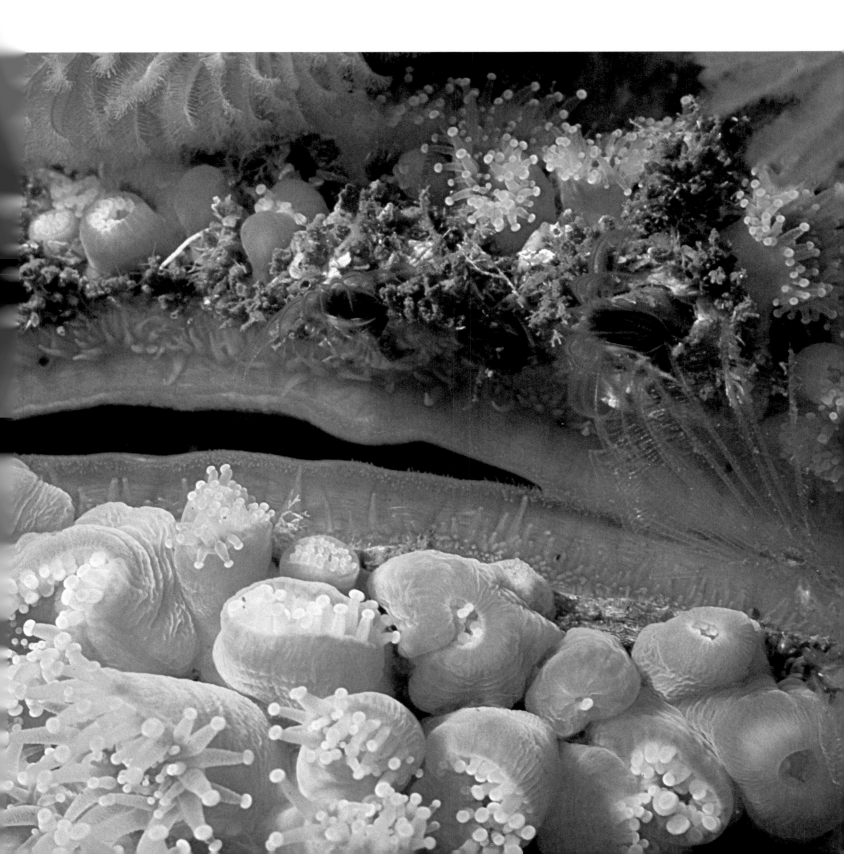

JOINTED LEGS
WITH SENSITIVE ANTENNAE

The arthropods ("jointed legs"), the largest group of animals of land or sea, include some 400,000 species. Crustaceans, like the lobster, crab and barnacle, are marine arthropods. These animals have tough body coverings (hence the name *crustacea*) and almost all of them, with the exception of the barnacle, are mobile. A barnacle attaches itself to a solid substrate, grows a hard volcano-shaped shell, and stays in the same spot all its life. Most crustaceans breathe through gills that are attached to their legs. Their eyes are black beads that protrude on horny stalks from the top of the head. Crustaceans use two pairs of sensory antennae as feelers; one pair is long, the other short. These are,

Below: ROCK CRABS (*Cancer antennarius*)
Opposite top: CANCER CRABS (*Cancer anthonyi*)
Opposite below: SPINY LOBSTER (*Panulirus interruptus*)

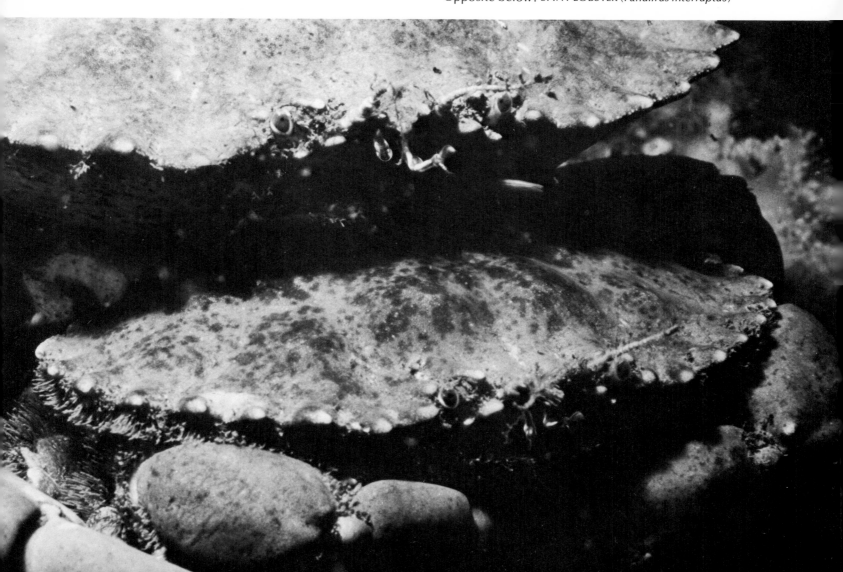

in fact, a more effective alarm system than their eyes.

Cancer crabs have the typical shape that most people associate with crabs. It is the big species of these crabs that are sold in markets. *Cancer anthonyi* is a brownish red crab, which fights pugnaciously for its territory. After two rock crabs (*Cancer antennarius*) have mated, the female carries the eggs near the abdomen. When hatched, the young larvae drift with the plankton.

The spiny lobster (*Panulirus interruptus*) hides in the reef's dark holes by day and ventures out to feed by night. This West coast lobster is a much sought-after delicacy. Unlike the East coast, or Maine, lobster it does not have giant front claws.

The sheep crab (*Loxorhynchus grandis*) is another crab that carries living things around on its back to camouflage itself. It uses living barnacles, invertebrates, seaweed and algae; some individuals are so covered with growth that they don't look like crabs at all. The sheep crab favors deep water kelp areas, though it has also been found in shallow water, notably under wharves. *Loxorhynchus* means "slanting beak," and describes the nose of the crab: *grandis* refers to its big size—this is the largest crab of southern California, with a leg span that can reach 40 inches. It is thought that those individuals of the species that are particularly large don't engage in camouflaging, or "masking," practices.

The sharp-nosed crab (*Scyra acutifrons*) is adept at camouflage; it plucks vegetative growth from its

environment and places it on its back where the vegetation continues to grow. By doing this, the animal is well hidden. Our pictured crab has chosen to hide under a yellow sponge; if it goes to another spot on the reef, it may pull off that sponge and replace it with whatever grows in its new surroundings. Because of this camouflaging habit, the crab is sometimes called a "decorator crab," though there are a number of crab species that transplant living things onto their backs in order to hide. The common name of this crab comes from its two horns that protrude from a beak. In Latin, *acut* means "sharp" and *frons* mean "forehead," and describes this particular characteristic of the crab. *Scyra* means "rough," and refers to the back of the animal, which is bumpy and irregular.

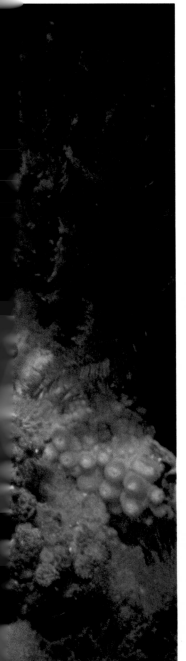

Opposite: SHEEP CRAB (*Loxorhynchus grandis*)
Below: SHARP-NOSED CRAB (*Scyra acutifrons*)

A SHELTERING FOREST
FOR ANIMALS AND PLANTS

The backbone of a temperate Pacific coast reef is usually the kelp bed. The towering stalks of this giant brown seaweed (*Macrocystis pyrifera*) form a sheltering forest for fish and invertebrates in a water column that might otherwise be uninhabitable. Old-time horror stories to the contrary, kelp is not a trap waiting to devour swimmers and divers but, in reality, an important, as well as beautiful, marine habitat for thousands upon thousands of sea animals. Sea urchins, abalone, crabs, snails and fish all depend on the food this seaweed supplies. Its big holdfasts—round, rootlike structures—are nurser-

ies for sea urchins, worms, brittle stars and octopuses and the blades of the plant provide a healthy surface on which small plants and animals can propagate and grow.

Generally, seaweed does not grow on a sandy bottom. It is more likely to be found in a reef area that offers irregular, jagged rocks to which the plant can attach itself. Kelp can reach an impressive height of more than 150 feet, but its beauty is most striking at the water's surface, where its branches spread out to form a protective canopy that effectively stills the wind and shields the animals below.

Below: KELP (*Macrocystis pyrifera*)
Opposite: KELP (*Macrocystis pyrifera*)

The submarine forest that is created by kelp plants would not be possible were it not for little gas-filled bulbs, or floats (pneumatocysts), which hold up the long stems—called stipes—of the plant. One gas inside these bulbs is carbon dioxide. The blades of the giant kelp, on which animals such as mussels or barnacles grow, could easily become overloaded by their weight despite these gas-filled floats. But the individual blades of the kelp deteriorate in just one or two months, which gives these animals no time to begin growing on the blades. Although, at times, older blades will be encrusted with little animals, little mossy bryozoans, these animals weigh very little, are spread thinly over the blade and serve as food for the many other animals living among the kelp. A dense kelp forest is a healthy haven of life, and some canopies at the surface spread so thickly that they block out almost all the sunlight below.

Some animals that seek refuge within the shelter

Below: CLOSE-UP OF KELP (*Macrocystis pyrifera*)
Opposite: GIANT KELPFISH (*Heterostichus rostratus*)

of the kelp forest are masters of disguise. They can transform themselves into a likeness of the plant they hide in. The giant kelpfish (*Heterostichus rostratus*) is such a camouflage artist. In kelp it will take on the brown of kelp, while in eelgrass it becomes bright green with silver stripes. Its range of color adaptability goes from shades of red to coral or brown, green or purple, all in accordance with its chosen habitat or its mood. This fish relies on vegetative environment for almost every need. It eats the tiny crustaceans found in kelp, where they have settled after leaving the plankton. It lays its eggs on kelp blades. During the spawning process, the male kelpfish takes up babysitting, swimming nervously back and forth over the eggs to aerate them and also to guard them from predators.

LONG-LIVED CREATURES
OF THE WORLD OF THE REEF

Fishes are the most prominent residents of any reef. Many are territorial, picking out their chosen nests and chasing off intruders. Others are camouflagers, able to change their colors to match their surroundings. And most fishes arrive at the reef as floating larvae and stay on in the community after growing up.

Most non-pelagic fish that live on plankton stay close to the shelter of the reef most of the time. However, when it comes to feeding time, they band together in large schools, hang suspended in midwater, and face the currents to pick out the plankton. Their planktonic meals include larval crustaceans such as mysids, amphipods and isopods. This school of blue rockfish (*Sebastes mystinus*) feeds at a depth of 90 feet. At night, they retreat to protective holes or ledges in the reef and there they become torpid or sleepy. Rockfish are among the most common type of fish off the Pacific coast; fifty-two species are found in offshore waters from the Gulf of California to Alaska. These fish are characterized by sharp dorsal and anal spines and have bodies shaped somewhat like bass. Very often they are called "rockcod," but they have no resemblance whatever to the cod family, Gadidae. Some

species live in water as deep as 150-200 feet, and others in shallow, rocky places. All rockfish give birth to living young. Their mating season takes place during the winter months, and inch-long juveniles are commonly seen from April through August. They normally live to a ripe old age, in the opinion of some ichthyologists as much as 20 years, and they have been in the historical picture for many millions of years. Fossil earbones (otoliths) of several kinds of rockfish have been found in a 12 to 20 million year-old deposit near San Diego.

The convictfish (*Oxylebius pictus*) owes its name to its characteristic red stripes. It is a shy, pointy-nosed fish that rarely strays far from its rocky hideout. It is small, just barely 7 inches long, and is preyed upon by the bigger bass and rockfish. The long nose of this creature is especially adapted to pick out little organisms from cracks and crevices. When the convictfish spawns, the female lays clusters of orange eggs among low-growing algae on top of rocks. The male then guards them from predators, swimming back and forth, rushing at intruders with a courage that is fantastic for such a little fish.

Opposite: BLUE ROCKFISH (*Sebastes mystinus*)
Below: CONVICTFISH (*Oxylebius pictus*)

Rockfish are among the most abundant types of fish on a California reef, though many of them live in deep water. The Scorpaenidae (rockfish) family contains at least sixty species, many of them difficult to distinguish except by color. The black-and-yellow rockfish (*Sebastes chrysomelas*) is solitary and hides in rocky holes. The fish is named for its color—a dark brown or black, blotched with yellow. The word *chryso* means "gold" and *melas* means "black" in Greek.

The cabezon (*Scorpaenichthys marmoratus*) is a guardian of eggs, a sentinel fish that sits on the bottom, always near its potential brood. This fish is a type of sculpin, a family noted for its characteristic big, bony head. In fact, the word *cabezon* means "large head" in Spanish.

While the black-and-yellow rockfish was named for its color, the kelp rockfish is named for where it lives: in kelp. It also lives in soft corals, aligning itself next to either one with head up or head

down, staying completely motionless. While the fish is in this trancelike state, a diver could conceivably go up to it and hit it on the head; because of this the fish has sometimes been called "dumb bass." There is no connection to the bass family at all, though rockfish do have basslike bodies. This particular rockfish looks very much like many of the other species of rockfish found off California, rather drab in color. The kelp rockfish can be distinguished by the series of sharp spines on the head, which resemble a crown; these are called coronal spines and can be a hazard to fishermen attempting to handle the rockfish on a line. The kelp rockfish is found from Baja California to San Francisco. It is most abundant from Point Conception south in about 35 feet of water, although it has been recorded to 150 feet. It feeds primarily in midwater and in the kelp canopy.

Opposite top: CABEZON (*Scorpaenichthys marmoratus*)
Opposite bottom: KELP ROCKFISH (*Sebastes atrovirens*)
Below: BLACK-AND-YELLOW ROCKFISH (*Sebastes chrysomelas*)

AT THE TIDELINE

THE TEMPESTUOUS REALM
OF THE RHYTHMIC TIDES

In the area of the tides, the shore takes such a beating that it is sometimes difficult to imagine how any creature, big or small, could survive in such a tempestuous realm. Yet there are thousands of living things that adjust their very existence to the ebb and flow of the sea. The sea itself has had a most significant role in the geological history of the planet. With every wave that breaks, the powerful forces of erosion are at work—tearing, taking away, shaping and rebuilding. It is a wonder that anything as mighty can carve such delicate patterns in rock or sand. The shoreline is a bit like time—never the same from one moment to the next, never duplicated tomorrow.

Often an intricate pattern is a combination of water and geology. This geometrically formed rock

Previous pages: POINT BENNETT, SAN MIGUEL ISLAND
Below top: ERODED ROCK SURFACE
Below bottom: GOOSENECK BARNACLE (*Pollicipes polymerus*)
Opposite: SOUTHERN PALM KELP (*Eisenia arborea*)

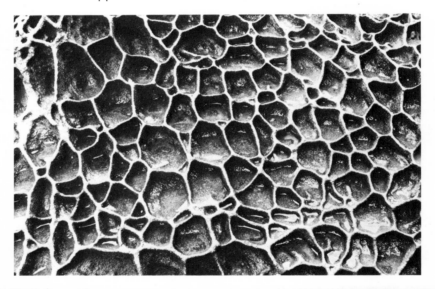

was originally a solid sandstone mass, interlaced with veins of a harder material. Over the years, the ocean beat against the rock, wearing away the softer sandstone and leaving the hard veins, exposed in a honeycomb network of stone.

The gooseneck barnacle (*Pollicipes polymerus*), a common tidepool animal, differs from its smaller volcano-shelled brothers because it has a long, flexible peduncle, or stem. These barnacles get their name from their long necks, which give them a slight resemblance to geese. In a symbiotic relationship with a limpet, the barnacle is being cleansed of adhering algae while the limpet eats them.

The tidal area of the reef is the most difficult of habitats for marine life. The ebb and flow of the ocean is life-water that is given and taken away from the tidepools. Yet many, many species have adapted to this on-again, off-again existence where one minute the sea is in and the next, out. Many people have learned something on their own about tidepools. They have watched anemones and barnacles on dry rocks, waiting for the next tide to feed them, and little crabs scurrying about, dashing from one shelter to the next. They have seen mussels, exposed to air and daylight, close up tight and barnacles shut their little trap doors until the waves come once again.

The hermit crab (*Paguristes bakeri*) is an amusing little animal that crawls around with a big, borrowed home of a seashell on its back. Unlike its more free-moving relatives, this crab never develops a hard, protective shell, so it picks out an abandoned mollusk shell whose original occupant has died, and moves in. As the crab grows, it will move into larger accommodations as it needs to. It crawls out of the old home, climbs into the new one, fastens itself to it with a rear-end pair of hooklike claws, and then it is business as usual. Hermit crabs are carnivorous scavengers and are known to engage in nasty battles with each other. Sometimes the victor will eat his adversary.

The giant green anemone (*Anthopleura xanthogrammica*) is a common tidepool animal that is a good illustration of symbiosis in action. This anemone gets its color from the green algae that lives inside the animal. The algae feeds on the waste products and leftover food from the filter-feeding anemone, and in return provides oxygen to the anemone through its process of photosynthesis. The giant green anemone is one of the few anemones that can live in direct sunlight. The green anemones from deeper water are not so green, because sunlight is greatly filtered at depth, and with low light levels, the process of photosynthesis is greatly reduced for the algae.

Below: HERMIT CRAB (*Paguristes bakeri*)
Opposite: GIANT GREEN ANEMONE (*Anthopleura xanthogrammica*)

LIFE
ABOVE WATER

A FORMIDABLE FIGHTER
OF THE CALIFORNIA COAST

Baby elephant seals twirling and playing with seaweed, young sea lions splashing in tidepools, old bulls fighting bloody battles at the water's edge, seals sunning and snoozing in the sand—all to the accompaniment of constant barking: this is the atmosphere of a sea mammal rookery. Isolated rocks, offshore islands, untrodden beaches where surrounding reefs support good fish and marine life—these are the places where pinnipeds establish their broods.

Pinnipeds ("fin-footed ones") are seals and sea lions; *pinnipedia* refers to the fact that the onetime limbs of the animal have been modified into flippers or "pinnas." These sea animals are an important part of the reef community since they rely heavily on the reef for food. There are two families of pinnipeds—the eared seals (Otariidae) and the true seals (Phocidae). The eared seals have an external ear and hind flippers that can be turned forward for propulsion on land. In water, they swim mainly with their front flippers. Sea lions and fur seals belong in this category. True seals do not have external ears and cannot use their hind flippers for forward propulsion on land. They do, however, use them for swimming. Into this group fall harbor seals and elephant seals.

Previous pages: CALIFORNIA SEA LIONS ON SAN MIGUEL ISLAND
Below: ELEPHANT SEAL (*Mirounga angustirostris*)
Opposite: ELEPHANT SEAL (*Mirounga angustirostris*)

In the early 1800's, furs and hides of ocean mammals became so profitable that a "gold rush" for their skins began. Hunters from all over the world, Russians, English, Aleutians and Americans, came by the boatload to the offshore islands of California and captured huge numbers of sea mammals. Great herds of seals and sea lions were slaughtered to the point of near-extinction until, in the late 1800's, some species were thought to be totally exterminated. When the noted mammalogist Charles Melville Scammon tried to piece together a population census for seals and sea lions in 1874, he reported that the pinnipeds were "in a state of chaos and collapse." At the end of the nineteenth century, the United States and Mexican governments extended at least partial protection to pinnipeds, and the populations of many species bounced back.

The Northern elephant seal (*Mirounga angustirostris*) is a formidable but amusing character of the California islands. Of the six types of pinnipeds that have made a dramatic comeback, the elephant seal and California sea lion populations have made the biggest strides. The elephant seal was valuable for its oil, but by 1860 it had been so decimated that it was too scarce to be of any commercial value. Because the animal can barely be aroused when asleep, it was an easy target for the sealers. By 1892 there were only nine left, a pitifully small remnant of a once-huge population, on Guadalupe Island. This tiny group, protected by the Mexican government in 1911, was the seed of the entire present population.

Elephant seals breed from December through March, the peak being January and February. This is the time when the great battles between males take place, with the giants engaging in bloody duels to gain supremacy over their harems. These are biting/shoving matches, and the loser will often be backed to the water's edge, at which point he will concede by plunging in. In contrast to such blood and tension is the breeding. Here, a pair of big elephant seals mate in the surf, he with his flipper over her. Peaceful, too, are the babies that learn how to swim and feed in the shallow tidepools.

Below: ELEPHANT SEAL (*Mirounga angustirostris*)
Opposite top: ELEPHANT SEAL (*Mirounga angustirostris*)
Opposite bottom: ELEPHANT SEAL (*Mirounga angustirostris*)

Seals and sea lions are especially made for the sea. Those who have ever seen a seal underwater will not easily forget the speed and grace with which they dive, circle, pirouette and loop. The harbor seal (*Phoca vitulina*) may be the friendliest of all the pinnipeds when it is swimming. Many divers have reported these spotted, bewhiskered seals tugging on a fin, peeking into a face mask. But on land they are skittish and will always stay close to water, taking off at the slightest provocation. This is because, being true seals, they do not have the locomotion of the back flippers and can't move too quickly on land. Sea lions, by contrast, will often stray far from water, waddling up on the rocks or sandy beaches.

Opposite: SEA LION (*Zalophus californianus*)
Below top: SEA LION (*Zalophus californianus*)
Below bottom: HARBOR SEAL (*Phoca vitulina*)

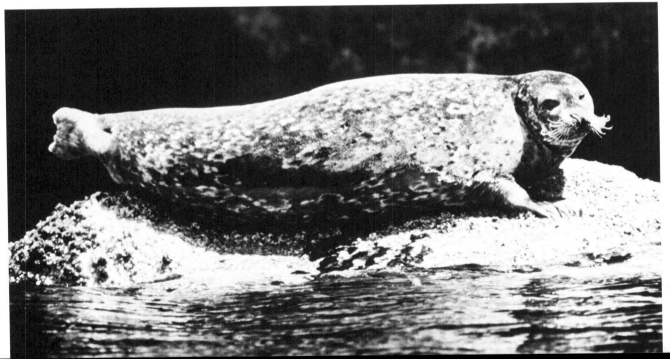

THE YOUNG
AND OLD OF A REEF HAREM

The California sea lion (*Zalophus californianus*) is the "seal" with which most dryland people are familiar. These animals are inquisitive, and many beach-goers have seen them swimming just offshore, looking around between dives. A large number of sea lions live off California, and they haul out to breed on the offshore islands as far south as Islas des Marias, Mexico, and as far north as San Miguel Island, California. For most of the year, the males stay north of the area inhabited by the females and pups. The breeding season begins in June-July, when the males migrate south to the rookery areas. In breeding, the sea lion male is highly polygamous, one male mating with several females. The males come to the rookery first, establishing their territories, which they guard very

Below top: SEA LION (*Zalophus californianus*)
Below bottom: SEA LION (*Zalophus californianus*)
Opposite: SEA LION (*Zalophus californianus*)

seriously. The females almost immediately give birth to one pup each, conceived during the previous breeding season; gestation is about a year. Usually within a few days of the birth, the female will mate with a bull. While the bull vigorously defends his own harem of up to fourteen females, the individual female is equally gregarious and will mate with more than one male. The rest of the time she sleeps, feeds or nurses her pup. The males do not eat during the breeding season. The growing babies gather together and play in small groups, trying out their flippers in the shallow waters just offshore. When the pups have matured enough to fend for themselves, then all of the seals leave the rookery.

COLONIES
OF ISLAND NESTERS

The total ecological picture of the reef would not be complete without a mention of the birds that nest there. There are many different kinds of sea birds, but without exception they all have one thing in common. The ocean is their main—and in some cases only—source of food. Each dawn they rise from their nests and, throughout the day, they dive repeatedly into the water to find their food, which is mainly fish. Every offshore island in the world offers a home to immense colonies of birds of many varying types and species. They nest in rock crevices or in cliff holes, their favorite roosting places always made evident by the white "guano" they leave behind. While some birds fly out from land to eat and others float or soar over the sea most of their lives, all birds breed on dry land. Hence, the importance of a reef.

Related to the snipe and the curlew, the sand-

Below: SANDPIPERS (family Scolopacidae)
Opposite top: MARBLED GODWIT (*Limosa fedoa*)
Opposite bottom left: CORMORANT (*Phalacrocorax pelagicus*)
Opposite bottom right: BROWN PELICAN (*Pelecanus occidentalis*)

piper (family Scolopacdidae) is a shore bird, which feeds on crabs and other small invertebrates. The marbled godwit (*Limosa fedoa*) divides its time between the shore, where it winters, and inland regions where it breeds. The cormorant (*Phalacrocorax pelagicus*) perches on rocks or floats on the surface of the water. It dives some distance underwater for its fish. When feeding, it often floats on the surface, then turns head-over-heels to swim underwater while chasing its prey. The cormorant has such a voracious appetite that the very word "cormorant" as an adjective is synonymous with "ravenous." The bird has a long neck and wedge-shaped tail, its two most telltale features. The brown pelican will dive from dizzying heights for fish, which it scoops up in its long beak.

When considering sea birds, one cannot help but think of their frailty in an ocean environment that is so often violent. But the birds are well equipped to deal with their tough existence. They are warm-blooded and their feathers further conserve their heat. Intensity of life is reflected in this as well as in a rapid heartbeat, quick breathing and a spare, muscular body that is so well adapted to the air.

A fantastic sight on a reef is the brown pelican, a perpetual glider, making a kamikaze dive for a fish.

It will soar effortlessly along, at a considerable distance above the sea's surface, until it spots its fish. With eyes fastened on the target, the bird suddenly tucks in its wings and falls to the sea with break-neck speed. The pelican rarely misses. The fish is snatched up in a huge beak and put away at one gulp. Right behind the diving pelican there will almost always be a gull with hopes of a few scraps.

The Western gulls feed by snatching quickly at surface debris, which can be dead or wounded fish

Below: WESTERN GULL (*Larus occidentalis*)
Opposite: PELICAN (*Pelecanus occidentalis*)

or any sort of food they can find. This debris consists of the carcasses of seals or sea lions, or sea animals and fish that have floated up on the beach and, of course, garbage. As scavengers, Western gulls are important cogs in the ecological wheel of the reef. These birds almost always fly in groups, filling the sky as they screech, dip and soar.

Few people have failed to be moved by the flight of a bird. Whether a seagull or a pelican, the bird knows how to take best advantage of the wind. It learns that it can get a lift by flying along the face of a sea cliff, where there is often a strong up-current of air. Once in the current, a bird can glide, with only the slightest movement of its wings.

Man took thousands of years to discover and to do what a bird has always done naturally. Even today, with our mastery of the air, we still look up to and respect—perhaps even envy—the ability of the bird to rise from the ground at its own will.

A GUIDE TO
REEF ANIMALS AND PLANTS

To understand the animals and plants in this book it is helpful to know how they are classified and the special characteristics of each group or phylum to which they belong. Once familiar with the biological particulars common to each group, you will be able to apply that knowledge to all animals and plants that fall within the same group.

INVERTEBRATES (Animals without backbones)

PHYLUM CNIDARIA: Cnidarians (formerly called coelenterates) are the flowerlike animals that have a body consisting of a small, elongated sac with a single opening, or mouth, surrounded by tentacles. There is a central cavity directly connected to the mouth for circulation and digestion. The tentacles of the cnidarian usually contain nematocysts, or stinging nettle-cells, which are used to poison or paralyze prey. (The word "cnidaria" comes from the Latin for "nettle.") The animals in this book that are included in the cnidarian designation are the hydroids, sea anemones, jellyfish, corals, sea pens.

PHYLUM ECHINODERMATA: Echinoderms ("spiny skinned") have a lumpy or spiny outer covering; those that seem smooth actually have little calcareous plates within the skin. Echinoderms have a system of tubes for water circulation and excretion. Locomotion is accomplished by tube feet. There are no terrestrial echinoderms; they are all found in the sea. The animals in this phylum include starfish, sea cucumbers, sea urchins.

PHYLUM ARTHROPODA: The arthropods ("jointed legs") include both land and sea animals; the sea animals are referred to as crustaceans, the name coming from their hard "crusts," or shells. All arthropods have hard body coverings and jointed legs. As the animal grows, it sheds its body armor, or exoskeleton, by a molting process, which it goes through periodically. After shedding the old shell, the animal will grow quickly in size, all the while secreting another shell from the underlying membrane. Animals in this group include the planktonic copepods and isopods, barnacles, shrimps, crabs, lobsters.

PHYLUM MOLLUSCA: In Latin, the word *moll* means "soft," and this is the root of the word "mollusk"—soft-bodied animals that generally have one- or two-valved shells, some of which are decorative and beautiful. However, some mollusks have little or no shells. These animals have a muscular "foot" that is used for locomotion; the mollusk gets its scientific classification from the kind of foot it has. For example, gastropods ("stomach foot") include snails (such as the cowry, top shell, whelk), sea slugs (such as the shell-less nudibranch), limpets and abalone. The cephalopods ("head foot") are those animals whose former foot has evolved into a head with useful tentacles. This group includes the octopus. The pelecypods ("hatchet-foot") are the bivalved mollusks, such as the scallop and mussel, which have two shells jointed together.

PHYLUM CHORDATA: The chordates are distinguished from the other animals by their notochord—an elastic rod of cells that forms the backbone, or axis, of their bodies. There are different subphyla that are distinguished by body types; one of these is the tunicata, animals that have their bodies enclosed in a hard, protective tunic. There are two large openings in the tunicates; one draws in water, the other expels water and filters out food. This group includes the salp.

VERTEBRATES (Animals with backbones)

FISHES (class Pisces): There are two primary groups of fishes: the true, or "bony," fishes that have skeletons of bone (Osteichthyes), and those that have skeletons or cartilage (Chondrichthyes). In the bony fishes, or osteichthyes, the subclass Teleosti include the great majority of all fishes. All of the bony fishes in this book are teleosts. The chondrichthyes, or cartilaginous fishes, include the sharks and rays (subclass Elasmobranch), whose skeletons may seem bony but actually are not. The fishes in the following guide are identified by reference to their specific families.

MAMMALS (class Mammalia): Marine mammals are warm-blooded animals that bear their young alive and nurse them after they are born. In marine terminology, they are sometimes called "re-entrants" because millions of years ago these sea animals once lived on land. Scientists point out that their bodies were once structured like those of a land mammal. An X-ray of a flipper shows the bone of a hand, wrist, fingers and upper arm. The mammals are subclassed in the orders Cetacea, Pinnipedia and Carnivora. Cetaceans are whales and dolphins (*cetus* is the Latin word for "whale"); pinnipeds ("fin-footed") are the seals and sea lions; and the Carnivora includes the sea otter *(Enhydra lutris)*, which is really a marine member of the weasel family (Mustelidae).

BIRDS (class Aves): There are twenty-seven orders of living birds, separated and identified by a combination of structure, geography and song. This book includes only a few examples of the orders Charadriiformes (shore birds) and the Pelecaniformes (aquatic birds).

PLANTS

Most marine plants belong to the group called algae, plants which have no true roots, stems, leaves or flowers. Marine plant parts have different names than plants on land. Roots are called holdfasts, the stem is called stipe, the leaves are called blades. The three major groups of algae are distinguished by color: brown (division Phaeophyta), green (division Chlorophyta) and red (division Rhodophyta). The kelps we talk about —the giant kelp *(Macrocystis pyrifera)* and the palm kelp *(Eisenia arborea)* are included in the Phaeophyta, or brown algae, division.

Opposite: JELLYFISH

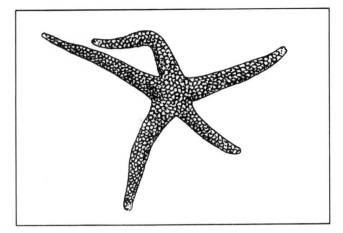

RED STARFISH *(Henricia leviuscula)*, phylum Echinodermata. A starfish of the family Echinasteridae, this animal is characteristically bright blood-red, though some individuals can be yellow or orange. It has long, sharply tapering rays. There are no pedicellariae on the back, but many little spines. This is a small starfish (6 inches maximum diameter). The females brood the eggs (January), keeping themselves in total darkness. The eggs are orange-yellow and are carried in a depression around the female's mouth. *Henricia* ranges from the Aleutian Islands to San Diego, California; intertidal to 100 feet. (Photo: Santa Cruz Island, 60 ft.) *Front cover*

CALIFORNIA MUSSEL *(Mytilus californianus)*, phylum Mollusca. A pelecypod ("hatchet-foot") that is very common all along the California coast, especially in the intertidal zone. It attaches itself to rocks or pilings by anchoring itself with strong byssal threads. In a typical mussel bed, mussels are found attached to anything, even each other. Tiny organisms live among the network of threads. The mussel is heavily preyed upon by starfish. It grows to 9 or 10 inches. To reproduce, the mussel discharges sperm into the water and also deposits at least 100,000 eggs annually into the sea. The mussel ranges from Alaska to California. (Photo: Santa Barbara Channel, 30 ft.) *Page 15*

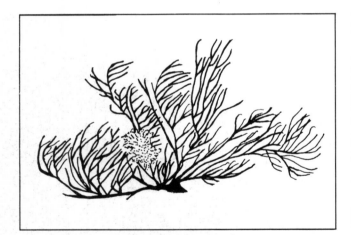

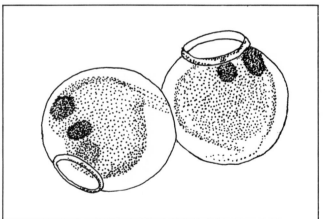

GORGONIAN CORAL *(Lophogorgia chilensis)*, phylum Cnidaria. Gorgonian corals are subclassed as Alcyonaria, colonial animals attached to a common stalk that secrete about their bodies a calcified skeleton. The individual polyps take in water and food and all of the polyps cohabit through canals that run through the entire colony. Polyps are of two types: autozooids, with the tiny stinging tentacles that take in food, and the siphonozooids, which have no tentacles but which keep water flowing in and out. They reproduce by sending fertilized eggs into water, where the eggs float with the plankton before leaving to form new colonies. Gorgonians are soft corals, two-dimensional animals that grow towards the prevailing currents. They face the passing water mass and the little tentacles of the animal polyps catch and paralyze planktonic food. (Photo: Gull Island, satellite rock of Santa Cruz Island, 40 ft.) *Pages 14, 27*

CABEZON EGGS *(Scorpaenichthys marmoratus)*, fish family Cottidae. The cabezon spawns between November and March, and the same adults usually meet at the same place year after year. The eggs are laid on hard surfaces that have been cleared of growth; they can number up to 50,000 from a 3-pound female to 100,000 from the 10-pound female. After the eggs hatch, the larva is a yellow-orange, covered with melanophores, or dark spots. The microscopic fish, only about 5 mm in length, resembles a tiny tadpole. It drifts with the plankton; at a more advanced stage, it can leave the plankton, settle on the bottom and grow into an adult. (Photo: Santa Barbara Channel, 40 ft.) *Page 16*

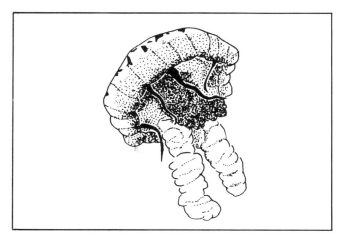

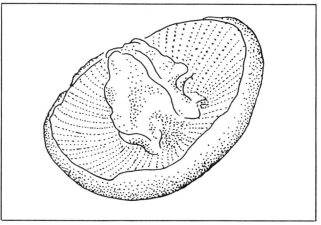

PURPLE-STRIPED JELLYFISH *(Pelagia panopyra)*, phylum Cnidaria. A jellyfish of worldwide distribution. Its pelagic, open-ocean habits are indicated by its generic name; the species name, *panopyra*, comes from the Greek words meaning "torch" and "fire," thus, "pelagic fire torch." The jellyfish is white with purple-brown markings and has eight evenly-spaced tentacles that hang 6-to-8 inches from the bell, alternating with eight sensory organs. The nematocysts within the tentacles are powerful and can be felt by humans. These long snares entrap and kill fish, which the jellyfish eats. (Photo: Santa Cruz Island, 3 ft.) *Page 19*

JELLYFISH *(Aurelia aurita)*, phylum Cnidaria. A transparent, pelagic floater that occurs all around the world, from polar regions to the tropics, often in huge swarms. The body is shallow, with a fringe of small tentacles all around the bell. From the top, one can see disc-shaped bands, which are the gonads. (Photo: Santa Barbara Channel, 3 ft.) *Page 21*

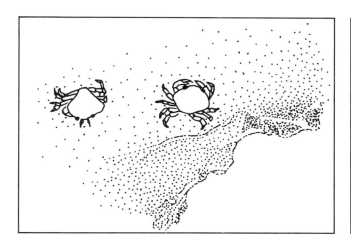

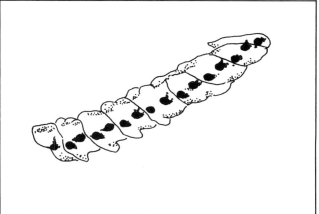

COMMENSAL CRAB *(Cancer gracilis)*, phylum Arthropoda. This crab ranges from the Aleutians to Magdalena Bay, Lower California. The legs of this crab are slender and graceful, thus its scientific name. Its color is tan with dots of red; full grown, it has the same shape as the big *C. magister,* the crab that is sold in markets. *C. gracilis* often travels on the bell of the floating jellyfish *(Pelagia panopyra)*, settling down on its gelatinous host during its planktonic larval stage. Here it grows and floats along, until the jellyfish reaches an inshore or reef area, where the crab hops off and begins its bottom-oriented existence. (Photo: Santa Cruz Island, 3 ft.) *Page 20*

SALP *(Salpa* sp.), phylum Chordata. A pelagic animal with a tunic body covering (thus called a tunicate). It occurs either singly or in long chains formed by an asexual budding procedure. The notochord, or rod that is the axis of the animal, disappears after the larval stage. Water, propelled in by cilia, flows in and out of the pharynx (that part of the digestive tract next to the mouth). This process brings oxygen to the animal and brings in microscopic plants and animals for food. (Photo: Santa Cruz Island, 1 ft.) *Page 22*

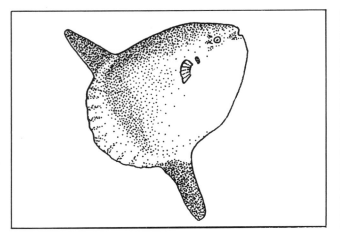

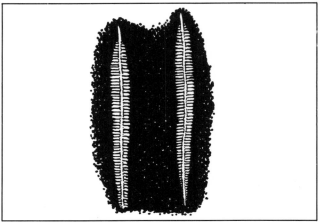

OCEAN SUNFISH *(Mola mola)*, fish family Molidae. The Swedish botanist Linne named the fish; *mola* means "mill wheel" in Latin, a reference to the round wheel shape of the fish. Like other plankton drifters, the mola mola is found all over the world—off Australia, around Hawaii (where it is called Kahala or Makua), off both sides of the Atlantic and in the eastern North Pacific where it is found from Alaska to well below the Mexican border. The mola mola grows to enormous size—a 4,400 pounder was reported off Australia. Maximum growth is normally around 2,000 pounds, but off California it will rarely exceed 125 pounds. The silver hide is scaleless, leathery, covered with slime. The young have jutting triangular projections, or spines, which disappear with growth. This fish eats jellyfish, ctenophores, crustaceans, small fish and pelagic mollusks. (Photo: Santa Barbara Channel, 10 ft.) *Page 23*

SEA PEN *(Stylatula elongata)*, phylum Cnidaria. These are feather corals (alcyonaria). Each colony looks like a feather, long and thin with the polyps forming tiny branches. The upper part of *S. elongata* can grow up to 2 feet in length, with the thick lower end buried in mud. The animal can contract and retreat completely into its hole when threatened. It is usually found at depths from 40 feet to 200 feet. (Photo: Santa Cruz Island, 120 ft.) *Page 26*

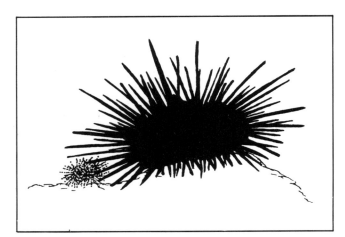

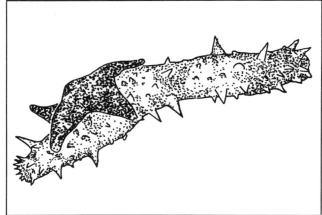

SEA URCHIN *(Strongylocentrotus franciscanus)*, phylum Echinodermata. This species is the largest sea urchin of the California coast, sometimes reaching 8 inches in diameter (though 5 inches is more common). The two-color phases are red-brown and dark purple. The generic name means "round-spined." The urchin moves slowly about on its tube feet, grazing on seaweed and algae. The mouth is on the underside and has five long teeth that meet in the center, a characteristic described by the Greek philosopher Aristotle, who likened the sea urchin's mouth to a lantern. Consequently, the jaw system has been called "Aristotle's Lantern." Male and female urchins are distinguishable by the color of their organs (white in the male, yellow or orange in the female). (Photo: Santa Cruz Island, 30 ft.) *Pages 24, 25*

SEA CUCUMBER *(Parastichopus parvimensis)*, phylum Echinodermata. The California sea cucumber is generally red-brown in color, with tough, leathery skin. The sea cucumber has no visible spines or skeleton, as do other echinoderms, but deep in the skin are tiny calcareous plates of varied shapes. The sea cucumber has a ring of tentacles around the mouth, which move constantly; some tentacles bend toward the opening, others extend outward. There is a continual pumping of water throughout the body. If disturbed, the sea cucumber can eject all its internal organs. The visceral matter is poisonous to predators and the animal can regenerate everything in 6-8 weeks. *P. parvimensis* creeps around on its many tube feet; the dark-tipped papillae all over the body are actually non-functional tube feet. (Photo: Wilson's Rock, off San Miguel Island, 130 ft.) *Page 26*

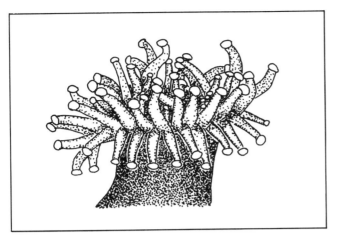

CLUB ANEMONE *(Corynactis californica)*, phylum Cnidaria. Also called aggregate anemone since it is a type of anemone that buds asexually and forms large, colonial aggregates. It is called club anemone for its distinct white knobs, or "clubs," on the end of the tentacles; *coryn* is a Greek word for "club." These contain the nematocysts, which are the stinging nettle-cells. The club anemone's colors are brilliant and can vary from white, pink, red, purple to brown; the tentacles are always white. These anemones range from central California to Baja California, intertidal to 100 feet, and usually grow in areas not in direct sunlight. They are common and in some underwater spots seem to carpet every available area of a reef or a piling. Colonial groups of genetically identical anemones are called "clones." (Photo: Santa Barbara Channel, 30 ft.) *Page 28*

BURROWING ANEMONE *(Cerianthus* sp.) phylum Cnidaria. Sometimes called tube anemones because of the large tubes which these animals build out of sediment and slime. The tube is interwoven with stinging nematocysts which stiffen it. The tube extends down into sand or mud and can be as long as 6 feet. The animal is free inside and can slide down to the bottom of its protective encasement. Otherwise, its tentacles extend into the water, to sting or paralyze. In the *Cerianthus* species there are two sets of tentacles, a ring of outer ones that are long and another ring near the center, or mouth, that are short. The pointed lower end of the animal is adapted for digging. (Photo: Santa Cruz Island, 60 ft.) *Page 29*

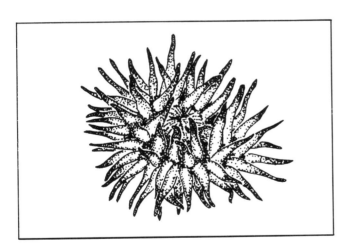

STRAWBERRY ANEMONE *(Tealia crassicornis)*, phylum Cnidaria. This is a solitary anemone with a circular stalk, or column, and an upper opening surrounded by tentacles. The base, or foot, of the anemone is called the pedal disk, and on this the anemone creeps slowly around from one spot to another (movement is slow, about 9 cm per hour). The anemone feeds by extending its tentacles into the water, and when they come into contact with prey (small fish or crabs), the nematocysts sting and paralyze it. These nettle-cells work by ejecting a kind of poison dart into the animal, which effectively stuns it. *T. crassicornis* is a bright red anemone, marked with specks of white or pale green. When folded up it looks like a bright strawberry, thus its common name. (Photo: Wilson's Rock, off San Miguel Island, 60 ft.) *Page 28*

HERMISSENDA NUDIBRANCH *(Hermissenda crassicornis)*, phylum Mollusca. This colorful sea slug is a mollusk that doesn't have a shell; in the larval stage there is a small, coiled shell that disappears as the animal grows. The word "nudibranch" means "naked lung," in reference to the fact that they do not have true gills. Respiration is directly through the body surface, or through what are called "secondary gills" (branchiae). The hermissenda nudibranch belongs to the Aeolidiadae family and is bluish gray to yellow green, with brown, red or blue cerata down the back. These dorsal projections are tipped with yellow. The animal grazes on hydroids; in the Aeolididea, the nematocysts are somehow processed through the body so that the animal has a stinging ability of its own, through the colorful cerata on the back. Common all along the California coast, from intertidal areas to 100 feet. It lays numerous white eggs in the hydroids. The life span of the nudibranch is about a year. (Photo: Santa Rosa Island, 70 ft.) *Page 30*

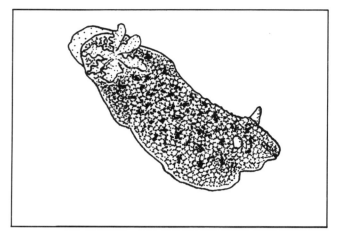

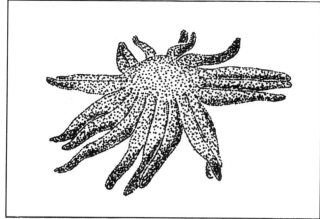

LEMON NUDIBRANCH *(Anisodoris nobilis)*, phylum Mollusca. This nudibranch is characterized by distinctive brancial plumes, flowerlike appendages near the rear end of the animal that are circular and can be withdrawn instantly. The back of the lemon nudibranch is rough and knobby. *A. nobilis* is bright yellow with patches of dark brown or black between the tubercles on the back. In the other species that are similar to *A. nobilis*, the dark markings appear on the ends of these bumpy projections. This is one of the largest nudibranchs, growing to 8 inches. It is found from central California to Baja California, intertidal areas to 100 feet, and is abundant from June to November. It lays its eggs in concentric, flowerlike configurations. (Photo: Santa Cruz Island, 30 ft.) *Page 31*

SUNFLOWER-STAR *(Pycnopodia helianthoides)*, phylum Echinodermata. This is one of the largest starfish known and is common along the entire California coast and north to Alaska. It can have as many as twenty-four legs, the young ones starting out with as few as six. The new arms, called "rays," bud out in pairs between the older rays until there are twenty to twenty-four of them. This starfish grows to 24 inches. *Pycnopodia* is commonly purple or blue, and sometimes also red, orange or yellow. The back is covered with tiny pincers (called pedicellariae), which keep the skin free of foreign external growths such as larval barnacles. The common name, sunflower-star, and the species name, *helianthoides*, refers to its similarity to the helianthus sunflower. It lives in intertidal depths to 100 feet. (Photo: Santa Cruz Island, 100 ft.) *Page 32, 35*

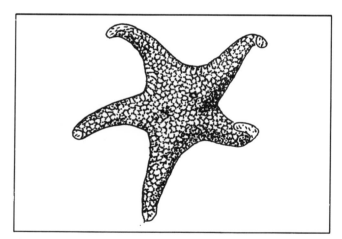

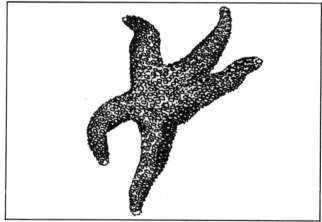

STARFISH *(Mediaster aequalis)*, phylum Echinodermata. This starfish, family Goniasteridae, is bright red and lives in deep water, usually 60 feet or more. It reaches about 6 inches across and has sharply tapering rays. It ranges from Alaska to Baja California. (Photo: Santa Cruz Island, 60 ft.) *Page 32*

GIANT SEA STAR *(Pisaster giganteus)*, phylum Echinodermata. Bluish brown with white spines that are ringed in bright blue. Pedicellariae (tiny pincers) are present. Grows to 22 inches and ranges the entire California coast; intertidal to 80 feet. All pisasters belong to the Asteriidae family. Like all other starfish, its main diet is mussels, sometimes barnacles and snails, jellyfish, detritus. In the case of a bivalved mollusk (such as a mussel), the starfish will open it by attaching its tube feet to both shells and pulling. This is rough work since mussels are very difficult to open. But the starfish has staying power and can apply pressure long enough to wear down the mussel. It only needs a crack, through which it can insert its stomach. (Photo: Santa Cruz Island, 60 ft.) *Page 34, 37*

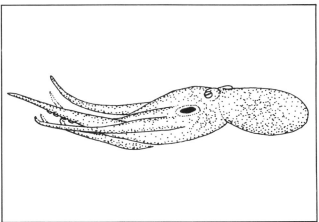

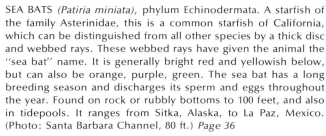

SEA BATS *(Patiria miniata)*, phylum Echinodermata. A starfish of the family Asterinidae, this is a common starfish of California, which can be distinguished from all other species by a thick disc and webbed rays. These webbed rays have given the animal the ''sea bat'' name. It is generally bright red and yellowish below, but can also be orange, purple, green. The sea bat has a long breeding season and discharges its sperm and eggs throughout the year. Found on rock or rubbly bottoms to 100 feet, and also in tidepools. It ranges from Sitka, Alaska, to La Paz, Mexico. (Photo: Santa Barbara Channel, 80 ft.) *Page 36*

OCTOPUS *(Octopus bimaculatus)*, phylum Mollusca. This is one of the most intelligent of all sea animals, very shy, in contrast to its frightening portrayal in literature; no doubt this reputation has something to do with its oft-used name, devilfish. By day the octopus hides, in a hole in the reef or a tin can or a bottle or kelp holdfast. At night it feeds on other mollusks such as abalone, clams, mussels. The female lays as many as 600 fertilized eggs in clusters on the bottom. These look like pale grapes. For four months she watches over them, cleaning and oxygenating them by forcing a jet of water across the egg mass. The scientific name, *O. bimaculatus*, refers to the two spots of pigment that resemble large eyes. These spots, just below the real eyes of the animal, have a dark center encircled with a bluish ring. This is one of the most common species of octopus off southern California (San Pedro to Panama). It grows to 20 inches in length. (Photo: Santa Cruz Island, 40 ft.) *Page 38*

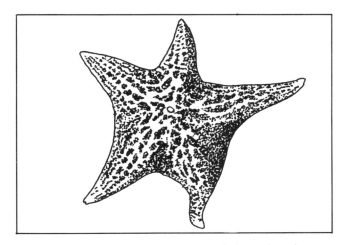

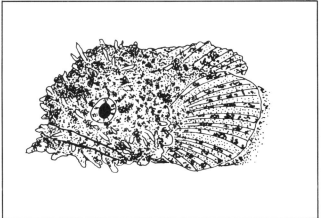

LEATHER STAR *(Dermasterias imbricata)*, phylum Echinodermata. This starfish, family Asteropidae, hasn't the bumpy, spiny backs of the other starfish; instead it is smooth and leathery because of a thick membrane that hides the spines. Colors vary between yellow, orange, red or lead blue, mottled with red. It is common along the entire coast of California, and as far north as Sitka, Alaska, to 100 feet. It grows to 8 inches. (Photo: Santa Cruz Island, 70 ft.) *Page 36*

SCORPIONFISH *(Scorpaena guttata)*, fish family Scorpaenidae. Although this fish is commonly called ''sculpin,'' this tends to breed confusion since there exists a distinct family of fish, Cottidae, to which the true sculpins belong. *S. guttata* is a rockfish, Scorpaenidae; it is sometimes called the spotted scorpionfish of California. Within the rockfish family, this fish can be distinguished by its numerous small cirri (fleshy, weedlike growths) that protrude from the head, snout and body—obscuring the fish against its weedy environment. It has numerous spines (more of them in young individuals), and they can inflict extremely painful wounds on humans. The scorpionfish is mostly red-brown in color and is spotted all over in green or brown. It grows to 17 or 18 inches and ranges from Monterey Bay, California to Cape San Lucas, California. It lives in moderately deep to shallow water. It prefers rocky reefs, but has also been recorded around piers, breakwaters and docks. (Photo: Santa Cruz Island, 15 ft.) *Page 39*

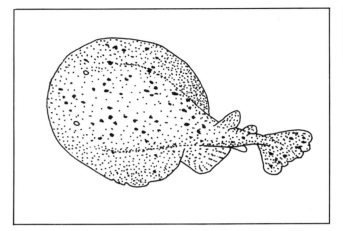

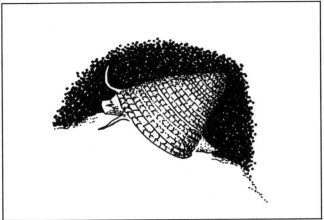

ELECTRIC RAY *(Torpedo californica)*, ray family Torpedinidae. Often called the torpedo ray, for its scientific name, sometimes called Pacific electric ray. This is the ray that can deliver a strong electric shock, which comes from muscles that have been modified into electric organs. It looks very much like the round stingray *(Urobatis halleri)* but differs in that it has two dorsal fins on the tail and no spine near the tip. The electric ray is bluish gray (sometimes a brownish gray) with black spots. It grows to 4 feet and a weight of 90 pounds, ranges from Sebastian Viscaino Bay, Baja California, to Queen Charlotte Islands, British Columbia, and lives in both deep and shallow water; intertidal areas to 640 feet. (Photo: Wilson's Rock, off San Miguel Island, 100 ft.) *Page 40*

RINGED TOP SHELL *(Calliostoma annulatum)*, phylum Mollusca. This is a small golden shell with whorls rimmed with beaded, spiral ridges lined with purple. The body of the animal is pink. It grows to an inch in diameter and is found from Alaska to San Diego, California. (Photo: Santa Rosa Island, 50 ft.) *Page 42*

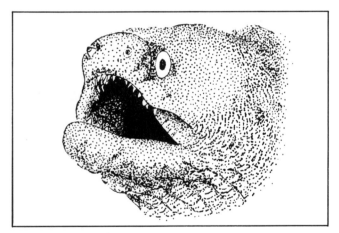

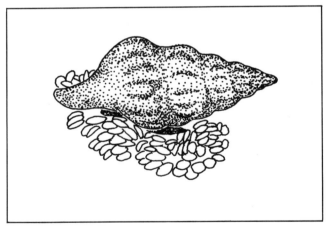

MORAY EEL *(Gymnothorax mordax)*, fish family Muraenidae. The moray is not a true eel but an eellike fish. The California moray has an extremely long, slender body that sometimes grows to as much as 5 feet. It is dark brown or greenish, with numerous small, white spots. The skin is leathery and scaleless, the mouth well filled with sharp, pointed teeth. The moray has a reputation for being ferocious *(mordax* meaning "prone to bite"), but this is no doubt due to its looks, and to the fact that as it breathes, the fang-filled mouth opens and closes. However, this is not to minimize the foolhardiness in reaching into a dark hole without surveying it first. A moray will bite in defense, but will not hang on as some would believe. By day the moray stays in its hole in the reef, coming out at night to feed on shrimp and mollusks such as octopus, mussels, clams. It ranges from Pt. Conception to Magdalena Bay, Baja California, and is most commonly found in rocky kelp bed habitats. (Photo: Anacapa Island, 30 ft.) *Page 41*

KELLET'S WHELK *(Kelletia kelletii)*, phylum Mollusca. This animal has a thick white or beige shell that is often covered with algal growths or bryozoans. Seven or eight whorls form a high spire with prominent knobs. Grows slowly and reaches about 6 inches. Said to live long; at 3 inches the Kellet's whelk is about seven or eight years old. Found from Santa Barbara, California, to Baja California; intertidal areas to 120 feet. (Photo: Santa Cruz Island, 40 ft.) *Page 43*

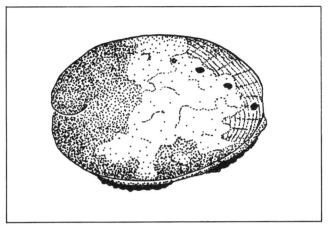

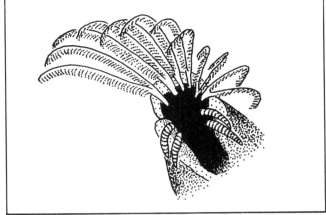

RED ABALONE *(Haliotis rufescens)*, phylum Mollusca. Of all the abalone species found off California, this is the largest—it grows to 11 inches—and most sought-after by commercial divers. The single shell is brick-red, interspersed sporadically by white bands on the outside, flattened and wavy, with a row of perforations near the left margin—about three-to-four raised holes which vent off the waste products of the animal. Along the edge of the shell are the sensory tentacles. A powerful muscular foot enables the animal to cling to rocks. The foot is eaten by humans as steaks, a popular seafood delicacy. The abalone grazes on seaweed, and ranges from Bodega Bay near San Francisco to Lower California, from shallow water to 500 feet. (Photo: Wilson's Rock, off San Miguel Island, 60 ft.) *Page 43*

BARNACLE *(Balanus tintinnabulum californicus)*, phylum Arthropoda. For a long time barnacles were classed with mollusks, until someone observed the larval development of the animal. Before the shell is formed, the little shrimplike larva attaches itself to a hard surface by the back of the neck, and then the shell is started. The barnacle will attach itself to just about anything. Subclassed Cirripedia ("feather-feet"), these fanlike feet extend out into the water, catching planktonic organisms. Then the feet quickly withdraw into the volcano-shaped shell, whereupon the animal eats the attached food. *B. tintinnabulum* has a red shell with vertical white markings and grows to 2 inches. When it is out feeding, the colorful cirri of red, white and blue can be seen (sometimes looking more orange and green). It ranges from central California to Baja California. Favored depths are shallow or intertidal, but extends to 40 feet or more. (Photo: Santa Barbara Channel, 50 ft.) *Pages 14, 44*

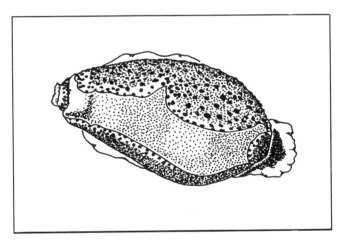

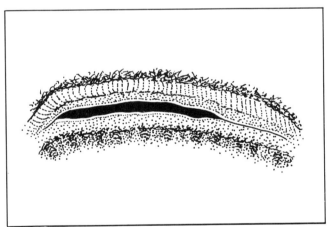

CHESTNUT COWRY *(Cypraea spadicea)*, phylum Mollusca, family Cypraeidae. There are many species of cowries throughout the world; most of them are found in tropical waters, but there are several species off California. One of these latter has a highly glossy, beautiful shell, and this is the chestnut cowry. The enamelled exterior is attributed to the polishing action of mantle, an outer tissue which is often extended out and over the shell. Juvenile cowries have a spiral snaillike shell; as they grow the lip turns inward and the spire is hidden by a layer of enamel. The cowry grows to 2 inches; its color is white beneath, a deep chestnut brown on top with dark spots and specks. It is common in rocky kelp beds and in intertidal areas to 150 feet. Ranges from Monterey, California, to Baja California. (Photo: Santa Rosa Island, 60 ft.) *Page 43*

ROCK SCALLOP *(Hinnites giganteus)*, phylum Mollusca, family Pectinidae. (Former scientific name: *Hinnites multirugosus*.) The pectins have rounded shells of the typical scallop shape and swim by snapping their way through the water. *H. giganteus* swims only when young; when it has reached 20-30 mm, it settles down on a rocky substrate to which it is permanently affixed. It grows a lumpy, irregular shell that blends into its surroundings. The left shell is flatter than the right. Inside, the shell is white with purple near the hinge. It grows 3-5 inches in diameter and ranges from Alaska to Lower California. (Photo: Santa Barbara Channel, 60 ft.) *Page 45*

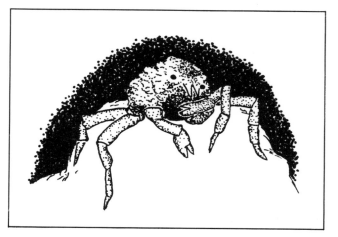

CANCER CRAB *(Cancer anthonyi)*, phylum Arthropoda. The Cancridae family of crabs includes nine species that are found along the coast of California. *C. anthonyi*, sometimes commonly called yellow rock crab, has a brown-red back and a yellow underside, and black-tipped claws. There are no spots on the underside. The crab is a decapod and can scurry quickly over the bottom on eight of its ten legs. The two front claws are reserved for pinching and catching. They move sideways, the legs on one side pushing, the other side pulling. These crabs often bury themselves in the sand with eyes and antennae obtruding. The females carry their eggs attached to abdominal appendages. When hatched, the larva is transparent and looks very different from the adult, with two long spines, one aimed forward, one backward, and two huge eyes on stalks. This mini-crab molts until it has evolved into adult form. (Photo: Santa Barbara Channel, 60 ft.) *Page 47*

SHEEP CRAB *(Loxorhynchus grandis)*, phylum Arthropoda. The largest crab of southern California, with a leg span of up to 40 inches. The carapace is lumpy and usually overgrown with bryozoans, barnacles or algae. It lives in deep water, along the coast of California to Farallon Islands. (Photo: Santa Barbara Channel, 50 ft.) *Page 48*

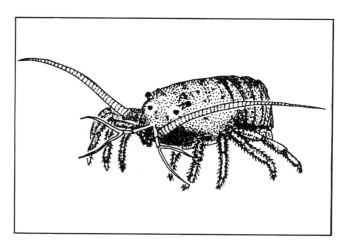

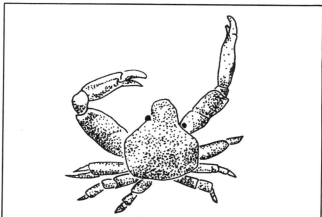

SPINY LOBSTER *(Panulirus interruptus)*, phylum Arthropoda. This is the prized catch of sport and commercial divers in California. The spiny lobster is red and there are spines over the carapace and at the base of the antennae. This lobster has no large front claws like those of the Maine lobster; females have small pincers on the last pair of legs, used in caring for eggs. In spawning (May-July), the female carries the coral-red eggs attached to swimmerets on the underside of the tail. There can be 50-800,000 of these; in mating, a packet of sperm cells is attached to her chest, and with her pincer-claws the female will transfer the sperm to the eggs for fertilization. The eggs hatch in 10 weeks. The lobster is known to grow to 3 feet and to weigh 30 pounds, though this size is uncommon. (Photo: Redondo Canyon, 150 ft.) *Page 47*

SHARP-NOSED CRAB *(Scyra acutifrons)*, phylum Arthropoda. The Brachyura are the true crabs, *Scyra acutifrons* included in this tribe. The common name comes from its two horns, or spines, on the beak. *Acut* means "sharp" in Latin and *frons* means "forehead," in reference to what looks like a sharp nose. This crab camouflages itself by picking sponge or other reef growths (hydroids, sponge, bryozoans) and transplanting them onto its back. Without its vegetative covering, the crab is gray or tan, with irregular bumps on the back (*scyra* means "rough"). It grows to 2 inches and is found along the coast from Alaska to San Diego, California; intertidal to 300 feet. (Photo: Santa Barbara Channel, 50 ft.) *Page 49*

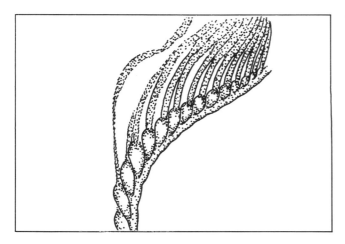

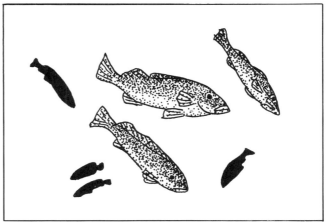

GIANT KELP *(Macrocystis pyrifera)*. The brown algae are plentiful along the California coast, especially the treelike giant kelp plant. This kelp provides an important habitat for many species of marine animals that alternately find shelter and food in its roots (holdfasts) and leaves (blades). Groves of these plants form an underwater forest in which fish find refuge. The holdfast offers a home to small urchins, worms, brittle stars, octopus. Snails feed on the blades. The stems (called stipes) can grow to a length of 200 feet and are kept afloat by pear-shaped bulbs filled with gas (oxygen, nitrogen, CO_2). Kelp is found anywhere from intertidal areas to a depth of 130 feet. (Photo: Anacapa Island, 15 ft.) *Pages 50, 51, 52*

BLUE ROCKFISH *(Sebastes mystinus)*, fish family Scorpaenidae. There are sixty species of rockfish on the Pacific coast of North America, all similar in appearance. *S. mystinus* is dark blue to gray above, fading to a white belly. All the fins are blackish. At night the rockfish retreats to a protective ledge or hole in the reef, where it goes into a sleeplike trance. By day it spreads out over the reef, midwater, in big schools, facing the current. It strains out small shrimp, mysids, amphipods, isopods and other larval crustaceans. Rockfish are preyed upon by albacore, salmon and hake. The blue rockfish grows to about 20 inches and ranges from Pt. Santo Tomas, Baja California, to the Aleutian Islands. (Photo: Wilson's Rock, off San Miguel, 100 ft.) *Page 54*

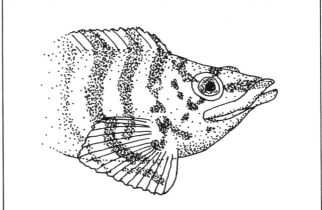

GIANT KELPFISH *(Heterostichus rostratus)*, fish family Clinidae. The Clinid is an eellike fish called a blenny (klipfish in California). It is characterized by a long, skinny body and sharp, pointed nose. The giant kelpfish lives in kelp, where it will appear brown, or in eelgrass where it will appear green. It can change its colors to match its surroundings; the ground color can be orange to red, brown, green or purple, with bars, blotches or stripes of a lighter color. Its range is from British Columbia to San Quintin, Baja California. It grows to 16 inches. (Photo: Santa Barbara Island, 15 ft.) *Page 53*

CONVICTFISH *(Oxylebius pictus)*, fish family Oxylebiidae. (Some ichthyologists class this fish with the greenlings, family Hexagrammidae.) The convictfish is characterized by a long, pointed snout and six or seven red vertical stripes. The anal fin has three or four hard spines, which, to other icthyologists, separates the fish from the greenlings. Above the eyes are cirri, fleshy protuberances that look like weeds. This fish grows to 12 inches and lives among algae and kelp from the Straits of Georgia (between Vancouver, British Columbia and the U.S.) to San Quintin Bay, Baja California. (Photo: Anacapa Island, 30 ft.) *Page 55*

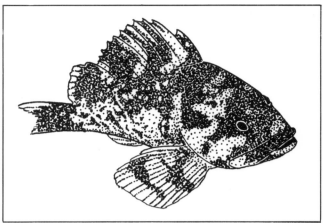

CABEZON *(Scorpaenichthys marmoratus)*, fish family Cottidae. The cottids are sculpins, fish that have large, bony heads. The word "cabezon" means "large head;" *marmoratus* means "marbled," in reference to the mottled pattern of the body. The cabezon has smooth, scaleless, wrinkled skin. Over the eyes are cirri —fleshy, weedlike growths that help to camouflage it against a seaweed background, as well as serving as a sort of sensitive antennae. The fish can change colors, becoming dark brown or red, tan, gray, greenish or nearly white. Individuals in an area of mussels can be very dark, those in a field of white *metridium* anemones nearly white. The fish grows to 2½ feet and 25 pounds and always rests on the bottom, except when it makes a dash to or from food, shelter, predators. It is a cold-water fish and ranges from Point Abreojos in Baja California to British Columbia (some scientists say Sitka, Alaska). (For information on the eggs and juvenile, see earlier reference, Page *16*.) (Photo: Santa Barbara Channel, 40 ft.) *Page 56*

BLACK-AND-YELLOW ROCKFISH *(Sebastes chrysomelas)*, fish family Scorpaenidae. Many of California's rockfish get their common names from their physical characteristics (colors, spines, etc.) or from their habitat or how they behave. This fish is named for its color—a dark brown or black, tinged with yellow. The word *chryso*, in Greek, means "gold" and *melas* means "black." This fish grows to 15 inches and lives in kelp beds and rocky areas from the shallow intertidal depths to 120 feet. It ranges from Natividad Island, Baja California, to Eureka, California. (Photo: Santa Cruz Island, 50 ft.) *Page 57*

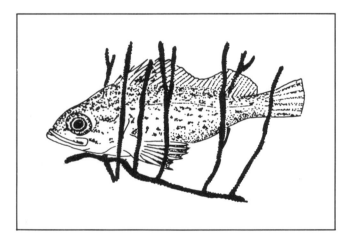

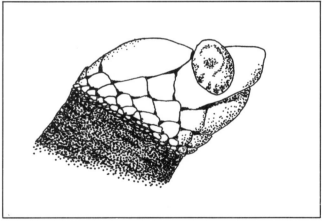

KELP ROCKFISH *(Sebastes atrovirens)*, fish family Scorpaenidae. This rockfish is named for its habitat; it most generally lives in the lower parts of California's kelp beds, lying near fronds or on rocks, or aligning itself next to corals in a state of stupor. This is possibly a camouflage mechanism. Rockfish have been popularly called rockcod, though they have no connection whatever to the cod family (Gadidae). The kelp rockfish looks much like other rockfish; it is drab—a mottled olive or brown over a pale brown background. There are sharp spines on the head in a crownlike configuration (called coronal spines). The fish is found from San Quintin Bay, Baja California to Bodega Bay, Sonoma county, California. It is most abundant from Pt. Conception south, in about 35 feet of water. The mating season is in winter; all rockfish give birth to living young. This fish grows to 15 inches. (Photo: Santa Cruz Island, 60 ft.) *Page 56*

GOOSENECK BARNACLE *(Pollicipes polymerus)*, phylum Arthropoda. (Former scientific name: *Mitella polymerus*.) There are reports of early naturalists believing that there were little geese inside the shells that today we call gooseneck barnacles, or goose barnacles. The long, fleshy necks of these arthropods resemble the long necks of the familiar bird. Like other barnacles the gooseneck barnacle is common from British Columbia to Lower California. The "neck," or peduncle, of the animal can be 3 inches long. Its color is red or reddish brown, with white plates. (Photo: Santa Barbara Channel, 10 ft.) *Page 60*

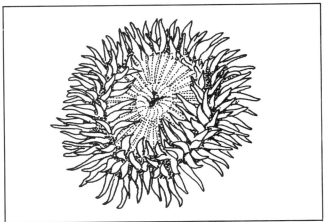

SOUTHERN PALM KELP *(Eisenia arborea)*, algae division Phaeo-phyta. So-called for its resemblance to a palm tree as it waves back and forth in surging water. It is found from Monterey to Baja California and from intertidal areas to 120 feet. Its stipe is short, heavy and divides at the top to support several blades that are narrow and long. (Photo: Santa Barbara Island, intertidal.) *Page 61*

GIANT GREEN ANEMONE *(Anthopleura xanthogrammica)*, phylum Cnidaria. A solitary anemone that can grow to 10 inches. Those in lighted areas are bright green, due to the symbiotic one-celled algae that grow inside the anemone. Those from deeper or darker waters are not so green because algae need light to grow. The anemone lives on rocks which are sometimes surrounded by or covered with sand. (Photo: Richardson Rock, off San Miguel Island, 30 ft.) *Page 63*

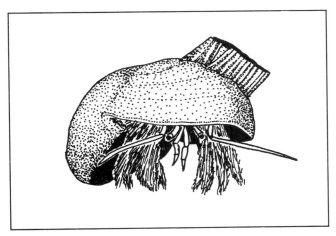

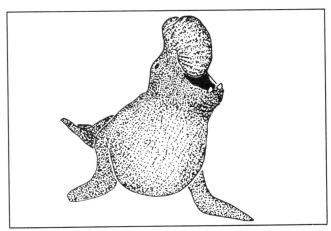

HERMIT CRAB *(Paguristes bakeri)*, phylum Arthropoda. Hermit crabs have large, soft abdomens and would consequently be very vulnerable to attack were it not for their adopted sea-shell homes. Their exposed parts are suitably covered with a protective armor. The *paguristes* crabs are distinguished by the fact that the sexual appendages are on the first two abdominal segments in the male and on the first segment in the female. In the closely related *pagurus*, there are no sexual appendages on the anterior segments. The eggs are coral colored and appear in January-March. *P. bakeri* is distinguished by the shape of the pincers—these are almost equal in size, spiny and with a straight inner margin. It ranges from southern California to Baja California, in intertidal areas to 80 feet. (Photo: Santa Cruz Island, 40 ft.) *Page 62*

ELEPHANT SEAL *(Mirounga angustirostris)*, pinniped family Pho-cidae (true seals; no external ears, hind limbs not capable of turn-ing forward for propulsion on land). The male develops the char-acteristic bulbous snout and can grow to 16 feet in length and to a weight of 6000-8000 pounds. The female does not have the prominent proboscis and reaches 11 feet and 2000 pounds. Adult males are dark gray above, lighter below, when they have their new coats. When the fur is being shed, it is brown. Females are darker. Breeding range is from Guadalupe, Mexico to Año Nuevo, California; the biggest rookery is at Point Bennett, San Miguel Is-land. Breeding activity is in winter months only, during which time the big males are aggressive and territorial. The rest of the time they are relatively docile. (Photo: Pt. Bennett, San Miguel Is-land.) *Pages 66, 67, 68, 69*

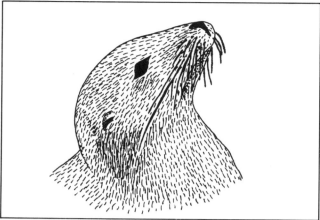

SEA LION (*Zalophus californianus*), pinniped family Otariidae (eared seals, with hind flippers that can be turned forward for propulsion on land). Full-grown females weigh about 200 pounds, males about 600 pounds. Both are dark brown, but females are generally lighter. Adult males have a crest of light hair on the head. Sea lions breed on offshore islands from the San Benito Islands off the west coast of Baja California, to San Miguel Island in the Santa Barbara Channel. After breeding (June, July) males move north to British Columbia. Bulls are noisy and territorial during the breeding season, holding their territories for 2 weeks or so. Single males may mate with as many as fourteen females. Two weeks after the first pup of the season is born, the female is bred. Gestation period lasts about a year. The young are nursed for as long as a year. They grow quickly and soon join a group of other young ones, playing on land and in shallow water. (Photo: Pt. Bennett, San Miguel Island.) *Pages 70, 71, 72, 73*

SANDPIPERS, family Scolopacidae. This is a large group of shore birds, including those commonly called curlews; most are white and gray or brown, with long legs and pointed wings. They feed along the shore, scurrying in and out with the waves as they poke about for crabs or other small invertebrates. (Photo: San Miguel Island.) *Page 74*

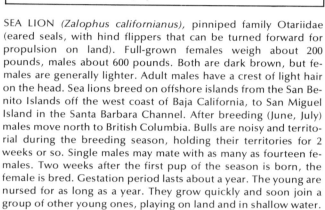

HARBOR SEAL (*Phoca vitulina*), pinniped family Phocidae (true seals). This bewhiskered, spotted seal ranges widely, from the arctic coast of North America to the southern shores of the continent. In the eastern Pacific it ranges south to Baja California. It is a common sight wherever it is found off California, but seldom seen in large numbers. The males grow to 5 or 6 feet and 250 pounds, females 4 to 5 feet and weighing less. The harbor seal is gray, spotted with black or dark brown spots. It can be almost black. Off California the young are born in March or early May. The pups weigh about 25 pounds at birth and are weaned in 3 weeks. It is believed that mating takes place in the water; there is no territorial squabbling or harem-type activity as with other pinnipeds. (Photo: Santa Cruz Island.) *Page 71*

MARBLED GODWIT (*Limosa fedoa*). This is a common bird in the west; it breeds inland and winters along the coast. Its feathers are a rich brown, mottled above and barred below. The bill is very long and upturned; this characteristic distinguishes it from curlews, whose bills turn down. The voice is described in the literature as an accented "kerwhit," or "godwit." (Photo: San Miguel Island.) *Page 75*

CORMORANT *(Phalacrocorax pelagicus)*. Commonly called the pelagic cormorant; a small *Phalacrocorax* of the Pacific coast, with a thin bill and slender neck. The breeding season runs from February through June. The nest is composed of a mass of seaweed, often perched on a narrow ledge of sea cliff. The female lays three-to-five pale blue eggs. The cormorant lives along coasts, in bays and sounds. The adult has a red face and throat pouch. It dives underwater for fish and crustaceans. (Photo: San Miguel Island.) *Page 75*

WESTERN GULL *(Larus occidentalis)*. The gull family Laridae is composed of strong, robust birds with long, pointed wings and a hooked bill. They are scavengers, feeding on dead things, flocking around garbage dumps and fish docks. They usually do not dive for food, as pelicans do, but will alight on the water to snatch something to eat. The Western gull is common and is recognizable for its very dark back and wings that contrast with snowy white underparts. This bird lives along the coast, in estuaries, on beaches, piers and in waterfront cities. It nests in grass or on cliffs on offshore islands. Females lay two-to-three spotted eggs. (Photo: San Miguel Island.) *Page 76*

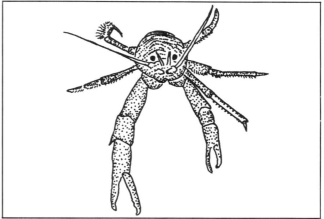

BROWN PELICAN *(Pelecanus occidentalis)*. The Pelecanidae are huge water birds with big throat pouches. They fly in orderly flocks and plunge, bill-first, up to 30 feet into the sea for fish and crustaceans. The adult brown pelican is dark with much white about the head and neck. The juvenile has a dark head but whitish underparts. The bird breeds along the coast to Pt. Lobos, Monterey, California, and on the Santa Barbara Channel Islands. Nests are made on the ground in a colony, where the females lay two-to-three whitish eggs. (Photo: Santa Cruz Island.) *Page 75, 77*

RED CRAB *(Pleuroncodes planipes)*, phylum Arthropoda. Since this crab resembles a lobster it is sometimes called the squat lobster. It lives in the open ocean, swimming or drifting in the upper currents, usually southwest of San Diego, California. Every few years, millions of these crabs are swept northward and ashore, where they die. It is a small animal, growing to only 3-5 inches; it is heavily preyed upon by tuna. (Photo: Santa Cruz Island, 15 ft.) *Back Cover*

INDEX

Illustrations are indicated by *italic* page numbers.

ELEPHANT SEALS

PELICANS FEEDING

BIBLIOGRAPHY

Barnes, Robert D. *Invertebrate Zoology.* Philadelphia: Saunders, 1963, 632 pp.

Borror, Donald J. *Dictionary of Word Roots and Combining Forms.* Palo Alto: National Press Books, 1960, 134 pp.

Cannon, Ray. *How to Fish the Pacific Coast.* Palo Alto: Lane Book Co., 1967, 160 pp.

Daugherty, Anita E. *Marine Mammals of California.* State of California Dept. of Fish and Game, Sacramento: 1965, 87 pp.

Fitch, John E., and Lavenberg, Robert J. *Marine Food and Game Fishes of California.* Berkeley: University of California Press, 1971, 179 pp.

————. *Tidepool and Nearshore Fishes of California.* Berkeley: University of California Press, 1975, 156 pp.

Galbraith, Robert, and Boehler, Ted. *Subtidal Marine Biology of California.* Happy Camp, Ca.: Naturegraph Publishers, 1974, 128 pp.

Hedgpeth, Joel, and Hinton, Sam. *Common Seashore Life of Southern California.* Happy Camp, Ca.: Naturegraph Publishers, 1961, 64 pp.

Hinton, Sam. *Seashore Life of Southern California.* Berkeley: University of California Press, 1969, 181 pp.

Johnson, Myrtle E., and Snook, Harry J. *Seashore Animals of the Pacific Coast.* New York: Dover Publications, 1927, 659 pp.

Light, S.F., et. al. *Intertidal Invertebrates of the Central California Coast.* Berkeley: University of California Press, 1970, 446 pp.

MacFarland, Frank M. *Studies of Opisthobranchiate Mollusks of the Pacific Coast of North America, Mem.* California Academy of Sciences, San Francisco: 1966, 546 pp.

MacGinitie, George E. and MacGinitie, Nettie. *Natural History of Marine Animals.* London: McGraw-Hill, 1949, 473 pp.

Miller, Daniel J., and Lea, Robert N. *Guide to the Coastal Marine Fishes of California.* State of California Dept. of Fish and Game, Fish Bulletin No. 157. Sacramento: 1972, 235 pp.

North, Wheeler. *Underwater California.* Berkeley: University of California Press, 1976, 276 pp.

Orr, Robert T. *Marine Mammals of California.* Berkeley: University of California Press, 1972, 64 pp.

Peterson, Roger Tory. *A Field Guide to Western Birds.* Boston: Houghton Mifflin Co., 1961, 366 pp.

Ricketts, Edward E., and Calvin, Jack. *Between Pacific Tides,* 4th Ed. Stanford: Stanford University Press, 1968, 516 pp.

Robbins, Chandler S.; Bruun, Bertel; and Zim, Herbert S. *Birds of North America.* New York: Golden Press, 1966, 340 pp.

Roedel, Phil M. *Common Ocean Fishes of the California Coast,* State of California Dept. of Fish and Game, Fish Bulletin No. 91. Sacramento: 1953, 184 pp.

University of Southern California Marine Extension Program. *The Island World of the Californias.* USC Extension Division Marine Science Affairs; Exploring the Channel Islands of California, Program III, 75 pp.

ACKNOWLEDGMENTS

The author and photographer are not PhDs or scientists, only people who love the sea. Therefore, this book would not have been possible without the patient help and advice of our good friend Shane Anderson, a biologist/collector with the University of California, Santa Barbara. If there are any mistakes in our text, they are ours and not his. Special thanks also to Vic Caliva, who spent many hours on the printing of the photographs that appear in this book.

TRACKS OF A WESTERN GULL